A Companion to the Gospel of Mark

MICHAEL B. RASCHKO

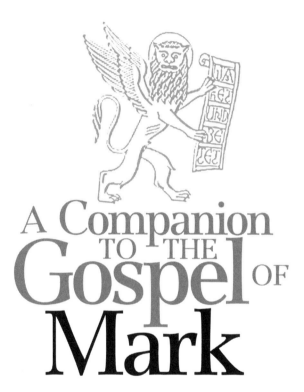

A Companion
TO THE
Gospel OF
Mark

TWENTY-THIRD PUBLICATIONS

185 WILLOW STREET • PO BOX 180 • MYSTIC, CT 06355
TEL: 1-800-321-0411 • FAX: 1-800-572-0788
E-MAIL: ttpubs@aol.com • www.twentythirdpublications.com
Bayard

Twenty-Third Publications
A Division of Bayard
185 Willow Street
P.O. Box 180
Mystic, CT 06355
(860) 536-2611 or (800) 321-0411
www.twentythirdpublications.com

ISBN:1-58595-279-6
Library of Congress Catalog Card Number: 2003108554
Printed in the U.S.A.

DEDICATION

To my father and mother
Vernon and Dorothy Raschko

ACKNOWLEDGMENTS

I would like to thank Father Pat Howell, SJ, a good friend and the dean of the School of Theology and Ministry of Seattle University. He gave me the sabbatical to write this book, asked how the work was going at appropriate times (a very tricky art), and generously gave the book its first edit. I would also like to thank Father John Topel, SJ, and Karen Barta, New Testament scholars at Seattle University, who gave the manuscript an early critical reading.

Thanks too to Father Stephen Rowan, who thoroughly edited the book and offered many helpful suggestions.

I very much appreciate my colleagues on the faculty of the School of Theology and Ministry and our many students. They provide a wonderful setting to do theology that is both challenging and well-anchored in the world of ministry. I am also grateful to the "canoe group," close friends and fellow ministers who respect and support my work as a theologian, but do not let me become lost in that role.

A small word of thanks to Haley and Maxwell Parsons, who, at the ages of four and two, have no clue what this book is saying but understand its central message quite well. Playing with them keeps things anchored in reality. A deep word of gratitude goes to their great aunt, Carol Ann McMullen, SNJM, my friend. Her ministry has brought life to many and is a great example of the themes in this book.

And last but hardly least, I thank Archbishop Raymond Hunthausen for his personal support of me in my role as a theologian.

CONTENTS

INTRODUCTION

Curly: None of you get it. Do you know what the secret of life is?
Mitch: No. What?
Curly: (Holds up his right index finger) This!
Mitch: Your finger?
Curly: One thing, just one thing. You stick to that and everything else don't mean ____.
Mitch: That's great, but what's the one thing?
Curly: That's what you've gotta figure out.

City Slickers, directed by Ron Underwood, 1991

The evangelist Mark and Curly agree on a key point: the secret of life is but one thing. The challenge is to discover what that one thing is. In the fourth chapter of his gospel Mark pictures Jesus saying to his disciples, "To you has been given the secret of the kingdom of God" (Mk 4:11). Unlike Matthew (Mt 13:11) and Luke (Lk 8:10), Mark uses the singular when he speaks of the secret of the kingdom. For Mark there is but one thing to learn, one mystery to be broken open.

Breaking that secret open, however, is difficult. For many Christians contact with the gospel comes primarily in the Sunday lectionary readings for Year B, and the lectionary breaks the gospel up from week to week into individual passages that get our attention. The gospel as a whole and how this particular passage fits in the strategy of the gospel fade into the distant background as our attention focuses on the particular story. Homilists may preach well on the particular Sunday reading from Mark, but the good news that unfolds slowly as the gospel progresses through the story of Jesus often eludes us for many reasons. Many homilists preach in a rotation. Unless all involved in that rotation coordinate how they want to develop the message of Mark in their preaching over year B of the lectionary, it becomes even more difficult

1

to let the theology of the gospel develop in their preaching. Nor does the structure of the lectionary always help. It leaves out key passages in its coverage of the second gospel. Sometime in August the lectionary drops Mark in the middle of a key section to read John 6. The feasts on the Sundays following Pentecost wipe out important passages, usually from the fourth chapter of Mark.

Outside the liturgy, readers, too, can have a difficult time getting at the core of Mark's message. As readers, we may concentrate on isolated passages. The overall structure of the gospel, in which individual passages find their meaning, is not obvious. That one central secret of the gospel, which every passage reflects, may escape us.

We are called to hear and preach the gospel, not just individual stories lifted out of their context. Those who gave us the current lectionary attempted to structure it so that we might spend a year contemplating the gospel of Jesus Christ as the evangelist Mark gives it to us. Mark has a message and a theology. It unfolds slowly as his gospel progresses, and each element in his telling the story of Jesus helps develop his proclamation of the good news and the secret that lies at its heart. Too often the current structure of the lectionary fails to foster such an approach.

Mark writes the whole of his gospel to help the reader crack the code of that secret. It is not an easy task. It takes sixteen chapters to look at this mystery from various angles and to explore the various layers of its meaning. The mystery unfolds as the individual reader, the preacher, and the congregation undergo a process of conversion as they move step by step through Mark's development of his theology. Even then the task may not be complete, for at the end of the gospel the angel at the tomb of the risen Jesus tells the frightened women to go back to Galilee, where the story had begun. If the mystery leaves you shaken or if you have not yet understood the heart of it, you must return to the beginning and work your way through the clues once again.

The mystery Mark puts before us must be broken open and solved, for the gospel proclaims a message we must come to terms with. But unlike other mystery stories, the mystery of the gospel continues to resist a final solution. For the mystery we confront in the gospel is the very reality of God at work in our lives. We do not so much grasp it, as it grasps us and calls us ever more deeply to encounter God, whose mystery is beyond our power to comprehend or to contain.

Clues to the mystery abound in this gospel. They range from the healing of a woman with a fever to the challenge of what we are to do with bread. They come in the form of parables. Rarely, however, do we get a direct statement. Mark does not believe that a direct statement of the secret will work. The reader and the hearer must be immersed in the mystery if it is to make sense. One must come to know it through one's experience. It runs too contrary to the world's wisdom to make any sense if it is just openly stated. Further, like all things of God, the mystery of the kingdom of God cannot be stated directly because it transcends this world. It can be approached only through metaphor, parable and symbol. So Mark approaches it indirectly.

Mark uses three techniques in this indirect approach. First, he places passages next to one another that we must interpret in the light of each other. The deeper meaning does not lie with one or the other passage but in the creative tension between the two. One of the more significant examples of this is in the eighth chapter where Jesus heals a blind man and then goes on to the discussion of the common perception of Jesus. Peter's inability to get any deeper than "You are the Messiah" is mirrored in the blind man's ability to see, but everything is still blurry. The blind man who still needs healing of his partially restored sight is Peter. What does he need to see to be healed? The passage that follows—Jesus teaching about the cross—is crucial.

This first of Mark's techniques makes interpretation difficult for the person who only hears the gospel on Sunday, the casual reader, and the homilist. Taking passages piecemeal Sunday after Sunday will not get to the gospel Mark is proclaiming. There is a connection between the healing of the blind man, Peter's incomplete confession regarding the identity of Jesus, and the first prediction of the passion. Reading or preaching each story as an isolated unit fails to catch the message of the sequence.

A second technique Mark uses is chiastic structure. A chiastic structure is like a sandwich in which the passages occur in a sequence of A B A'. The two A passages, which have some common theme, shed light on the B passage which they surround. The B passage usually bears the central message of the related passages. For example, the first miracle in Mark tells the story of Jesus casting a demon out of a man. The story of the exorcism is the B element in this chiastic structure. Mark has surrounded this story with references to Jesus' teaching. Jesus enters the synagogue to teach, and the response to the miracle is amazement at Jesus' teaching. We are not told what Jesus has been teaching, but the content of the miracle story provides an important clue. The teaching of Jesus is that he has conquered Satan in the desert and now has the power to drive evil out of our lives.

Mark also uses longer chiastic structures. He can have five elements that move in the pattern A B C B' A', or seven elements in the pattern A B C D C' B' A'. In each case the central passage bears the message of the whole pattern, and the paired stories illustrate it.

Finally, Mark's gospel as a whole has an overall pattern, although scholars disagree about exactly how the gospel is organized. Some see the gospel divided into two halves with Peter's confession of Jesus as the Christ marking the central dividing line. Others see the gospel divided into three parts organized around the three great statements that Jesus is the Divine Son at the baptism, the transfiguration, and the crucifixion.

I think there is a much subtler organizing principle for the gospel as a whole. Mark has organized it in layers. Each layer offers clues about the central mystery of the kingdom of God from a particular perspective. As readers begin to come to some clarity about the kingdom of God from that perspective, Mark moves on to a further layer that calls the reader more deeply into the mystery. The gospel is like a series of boxes each beautifully wrapped and each containing within it further beautifully wrapped boxes. Readers are immersed in the theme of the outermost box, and just as they think they have the secret solved, Mark says no, there is a box inside this one you must unwrap and contemplate. The gospel keeps moving more deeply into the reality of the mystery of the kingdom of God until it reaches its resolution in the climax of the story. If one has not come to terms with the mystery, Mark ends the gospel by telling us to start again where the gospel began in Galilee.

The structure of the gospel needs close attention if we are to unravel the mystery which it proclaims. Both the reader and the preacher must be aware of the kinds of constructions that hold various passages together. The clues to the secret of the kingdom often lie between passages. The reader must also be aware when Mark has moved to a new, deeper layer in his contemplation of the mystery. With each new box the questions that the reader and homilist are asked to address open a new perspective that the homilist especially must explore with the congregation.

However, the position the reader and the homilist must finally take up in relation to the gospel is not that of analyzing the structures of the text. Hermeneutical theory speaks of three strategies an interpreter may take in approaching the text. First, one may look behind the text. Here the attention of the interpreter is on the world out of which the text emerged. Various questions engage us when we take up this perspective: for what kind of community did Mark write the gospel? What was happening historically that may have shaped Mark's message? Where was the gospel written? Who was the real author of the gospel attributed to Mark? What were the actual historical events in the life of Jesus upon which the gospel is based? What was the mind and intention of the author in writing the gospel? These are the questions which the various methods of historical critical interpretation address.

Secondly, the reader and the preacher may concentrate on the text itself. Here they focus on the structure and themes of the gospel. They ask questions such as these: What is the overall structure of the gospel? What literary devices does Mark like to use to shape his message? Who are the key figures in the story Mark tells, and what is the plot line? Most importantly, they ask what kind of world the gospel presents and what way of being in the world Mark imagines is possible for humankind.

Finally, the interpreter can position himself in front of the gospel. Here one is not analyzing the world of the gospel or how the text is constructed. Rather, the world of the gospel and how the text is structured engage the reader and the homilist in such a manner that one begins to wonder about the possibilities in one's own world if the world the gospel projects is truly credible.

Taking up a position in front of the text involves three hermeneutical assumptions. First, the text of the gospel bears a surplus of meaning. This text is so rich, so full of potential meaning for the human community, that no one interpretation is ever able to capture and nail down once and for all the meaning of the gospel. We see something similar in the life of Jesus. His life is so full of meaning that we have four canonical gospels, each of which interprets the story of Jesus from a very different angle. The same holds true for each of those four gospels and the gospel of Mark in particular. The gospel of Mark did have a specific meaning in the mind of its author and in the world that originally received and read it. But neither the mind of Mark nor the initial reading of the gospel by his community can exhaust the possibilities of what Mark has brought to expression. As the gospel spread from its original setting and new communities read it from different perspectives down through the history of the Christian people, new meanings came to light.

Secondly, this surplus can give birth to a pluralism of possible interpretations of the gospel. However, pluralism does not justify a wide-open relativism or a tendentious reading whereby the preacher may impose whatever he wants or needs on the gospel. Some homilists can be quite creative in what they find in the gospel, but they do not always respect the gospel as a work that has an integrity of its own. The gospel itself as a work, with its themes, its structure, and the world it projects, limits the pluralism of possible readings.

The pluralism of possible readings of the gospel is rooted in the third hermeneutical theme which comes into play when readers position themselves in front of the text: the possibility of a fusion of horizons. The gospel presents us with an understanding of the world and a way of being in the world. If the gospel has any merit at all, this way of viewing the world ought to shake us to our foundations because the world that it imagines holds such different possibilities from the one in which we now find ourselves comfortable. It invites us to see differently, to imagine ourselves and our relationships differently, to engage reality in a way that reaches for a new set of possibilities. On the other hand, the world in which we live, the world of our everyday assumptions about life, brings a new perspective and a new set of questions to the text which medieval or nineteenth-century Christians could not have imagined. When these two worlds meet—the strange world of the text and the world of the interpreter—a fusion of the horizons of meaning of those worlds becomes possible. The perspectives and questions of the world of the interpreter open aspects of the meaning of the gospel that earlier generations have not seen. At the same time, the reading of the gospel reshapes the world of the reader and the homilist. The gospel opens new possibilities for human life because the imagination is able to see the world in new ways.

The gospel of Mark places before readers a new and different world from the one in which they normally live. It is a world where a small amount of food can feed thousands, where the evil that has come to possess people can be driven out, where a word can quiet chaotic storms at sea. It is a world where life can come from death. At its heart lies the secret, which the gospel seeks to reveal. The gospel calls the reader to a new world. Ultimately the task of the reader and homilist is to engage in such a fusion of horizons. If Jesus can expel the evil from a man's life in the gospel, what is possible in our lives? The gospel ought to shake the foundations of the reader's world and invite one into a world in which new things are possible.

In this book we will not spend a great deal of time behind the text. The search for the actual history on which the gospel rests, the effort to understand the mind of Mark, or the scholarly work that seeks a historical sense of the Greco-Roman culture of the community for which he initially wrote are all interesting and important tasks. However, they are not the task of the preacher or the person of faith reading the gospel for spiritual nourishment. Preachers and readers of the gospel of Mark need to take up the last two hermeneutical stances: within the text and in front of the text. They need to come to terms with the structure and themes of the gospel so that they might understand the world envisioned by the text. Then they need to stand before the text in such a way that the gospel opens new possibilities for life.

Hermeneutical theory overlooks one ingredient that is essential for a fusion of the horizons of the world of the gospel and the world of the contemporary Christian community. That ingredient is the work of the Holy Spirit. The Spirit works through the gifts and genius of the author, Mark, who has given us a text that bears such a wealth of meaning. And the Spirit works in the community and through the homilist who enables new dimensions of meaning and promises of life to emerge in a new reading of the gospel. Openness to the presence and work of the Holy Spirit through prayer is therefore essential if the gospel is to speak to our communities in the early twenty-first century.

Each chapter of this book will address one of the consecutive layers or boxes that make up the gospel and through which Mark slowly reveals the secret of the gospel he proclaims. Each chapter will first examine the literary structure and devices Mark uses and the world the text envisions. Then it will move from a position within the gospel to one in front of the gospel and examine what is possible for the Christian community today if the world of the gospel is true. It is there in front of the text that an applied reading of the gospel takes place.

This book has several audiences in mind. The first is preachers. Good preaching involves a fusion of horizons. It brings together the world the gospel proclaims and the world of those who hear in it a new set of promises for life. It offers a new way of understanding and being in the world. Thus I hope to break open the world of the gospel of Mark and bring it into dialogue with the world of the early twenty-first century. I have also written this book for those who would like to take a deeper look into the gospel of Mark without becoming overly involved in the technical study of Scripture.

I have written this book as a conversation about the themes of the gospel of Mark and a number of themes that are important in systematic theology. A number of friends have asked why a systematic theologian would venture to write a book on the Scriptures. There are several reasons I have chosen to do so. I am a homilist. I preach in a regular Sunday rotation in a Catholic parish. So I find myself often engaged with the text of the gospels. Like any other preacher I read a lot of material that comments on the text. The material I find most helpful is that which situates the particular reading in the larger context of the gospel as a whole. I also find it very helpful to bring in the themes I deal with as a systematic theologian. Too often the specialization involved in their academic disciplines keeps the biblical scholar and the systematic theologian from appreciating each other's work. Yet both are anchored in the same reality, the person and story of Jesus, the Christ. What ought to bring them together is the service of the community that seeks to be disciples of Jesus. This book hopes to offer of that kind of service.

Finally, readers of this book may notice that I use quotations from various translations of the Bible. I have done so because different translations emphasize themes or catch nuances I want to stress.

CHAPTER ONE

THE COMING OF THE KINGDOM

Mark 1:1–45

"'Tis still a dream, or else such stuff as madmen tongue."

William Shakespeare, *Cymbeline*, V.iv

The World of the Text

The opening section of Mark's gospel invites us to dream. It proclaims the powerful work of God in our world through Jesus and asks us to consider what is possible in human life if it is in our midst. Our dreams are not to be timid; they are to be bold. Our dreams must move beyond the limit of what our everyday, common sense view of the world tells us is possible. We are to embrace again the age-old hopes and dreams of the human race since the time of Adam and Eve; we are to look at the world through the visionary eyes of the prophets and to live the ancient wisdom of the sages. To the worldly wise these dreams may be "such stuff as madmen tongue," but if the kingdom of God is on the horizon, these dreams now become possible in a way they have never been possible before.

The dreams we are invited to enter are not simply those of the human race, or even of its great visionaries and seers. They are the dreams of God for creation. They represent what God had in mind when God first called this world into being. They embody the purpose of God throughout the history of God's saving work. The Scriptures use a code word for these dreams: the kingdom of God. The term is rather elusive, as all dreams are. Hans Küng describes the kingdom in the following way:

> It will be a kingdom where, in accordance with Jesus' prayer, God's name is truly hallowed, his will is done on earth, men (and women) will have everything in abundance, all sin will be forgiven and all evil overcome.
>
> It will be a kingdom where, in accordance with Jesus' promises, the poor, the hungry, those who weep and those who are downtrodden will finally come into their own; where pain, suffering and death will have an end. (*On Being a Christian*, p. 215)

Mark's gospel invites the reader to enter a world in which this vision is no longer the stuff of dreams, but a real possibility, for God is at work in our world and in our lives.

The first section of Mark's gospel consists of the forty-five verses of the first chapter. The heart of the section lies in Mark 1:14–15, a proclamation that the ultimate act of God in human history is taking place through God's Son, Jesus. This short passage is central not only to this opening section; it also provides the key to the whole gospel. In Mark's mind it is the gospel. Four quick clauses give expression to this central message: "The time is fulfilled, the kingdom has arrived. Repent and have faith in the good news (the gospel)." Mark shows the reader that this short passage is at the center of the gospel by placing it in the middle of a chiastic structure that runs A B A'. In so doing he inserts it between the repeated word "gospel," thus marking these four short clauses as a short, terse summary of the whole of the gospel message. The chiastic structure looks like this:

A The word "gospel."

  B The proclamation of the kingdom.

A' The word "gospel."

The two A elements are simply the word "gospel" which surrounds and gives a framework of interpretation to the central verse, 1:15. The central B element announces the presence of the kingdom of God. Mark structures the opening proclamation of Jesus in this way so that his reader will not miss the fact that these two sentences contain the controlling idea of the whole gospel. These two sentences, then, *are* the gospel:

> After John had been arrested, Jesus came to Galilee proclaiming the *gospel* of God: "This is the time of fulfillment. The kingdom of God is at hand. Repent and believe in the *gospel.*" (1:14–15, NAB)

The rest of Mark's sixteen chapters serve to unravel the meaning of these verses.

These first, crucial words of Jesus make a proclamation and call for a response. The proclamation is daring and radical. Time has been fulfilled; the kingdom of God is here. Mark emphatically insists that the kingdom of God has arrived. For that reason Mark turns his face to the future, for the end time and the promises it holds are already in view. For Mark the kingdom of God has arrived and already impinges on our lives.

This imminent reign of God calls for a twofold response. First, it summons us to repentance, to a radical change in the patterns of our lives. Repentance means changing not just our patterns of action, but also our patterns of thought. We must change the way we see the world so that we imagine what is possible. When something new breaks upon us, something new is possible. By changing the patterns of our lives, we seek to embrace the possibilities that God's kingdom holds out to us.

Secondly, this proclamation summons us to faith. By faith Mark means an attitude of trust and belief. Faith implies more than thinking the message is true or cleaning up our moral lives and living by the commandments. In Mark faith means living as if the possibilities the message proclaims are practicable. The gospel introduces a basic tension in the life of the Christian. The kingdom and the future it opens up are present and yet not realized. The response of faith provides the link between this presence, which holds such a powerful potential, and its realization. Jesus proclaims the kingdom and opens a way out of the present impasse in which humanity finds itself. But the promise is realized only when it is embraced in the lives of those who hear the message. Repentance and faith are not acts of preparation for the arrival of the kingdom. They are acts of response to the presence of the kingdom, acts that allow the proclaimed promises to take root and be realized in human life.

Mark invites his readers to dream. He challenges the people of God to live as if the promises of God were truly possible. He asks them how they must live if everyone is to share the abundance God created in this world; if there is to be forgiveness among human beings; if the poor, the hungry, those who weep and those who are downtrodden are to come into their own; if God's name is to be kept holy. In this first section of the gospel Mark has undertaken the daunting task of reshaping the imaginations of those who hear him as they think about their lives and their world.

The second passage upon which Mark builds the structure of his first chapter is Mark 1:32–34:

> That evening, at sundown, they brought to him all who were sick or possessed with demons. And the whole city was gathered around the door. And he cured many who were sick with various diseases, and cast out many demons; and he would not permit the demons to speak because they knew him. (NRSV)

This short passage is a Markan summary. Mark did not take this statement from the oral or written traditions handed down by the community but composed it himself. Mark uses this summary to draw together the themes he emphasizes in the miracles of the second half of the section and to tell his reader that such things were happening over and over again. Mark wants to draw our attention to the results of believing the gospel of the kingdom and changing our lives in accord with that good news. The kingdom of God dramatically alters the lives of those who believe. It makes them whole, heals them, and re-creates their lives. Mark stresses that great numbers of people came to believe the message of Jesus and that Galilee was flowering with the realized promises of the kingdom of God. Jesus makes those who were sick whole. Those plagued and captured by evil he sets free.

The section moves from the promise and challenge of 1:14–15 to the faith and resulting wholeness manifest in the miracles of the second half of the chapter. It proclaims the kingdom of God, the time of God's decisive action in human history, and shows the results in the lives of the people who have faith in the promised reality of that kingdom. The recreative power of God, present in and through Jesus, makes whole the lives of the people who have faith in what Jesus has proclaimed in their midst. The relationship of these two passages then serves as the foundation of the first section of the gospel.

The rest of the chapter supports these central themes with allusions to apocalyptic literature and expectations. These apocalyptic themes must have flourished in the community to which Mark addressed the gospel. The following are the key elements in the apocalyptic view that Mark incorporates into this first section of his gospel.

1. The apocalyptic tradition takes a pessimistic view of the human prospect within history, which has become hopeless. The Jewish people had suffered too many historical defeats and setbacks to hope for salvation within history any longer. The Assyrians and the Babylonians had defeated them. They had lived under the yoke of the Persian Empire. After struggling against the Seleucid and Ptolemaic successor states to Alexander the Great, they had managed to win their freedom for only a few short decades. Then Pompey and Caesar visited the near East, and the Jewish people lived under the boot of the Roman Empire up to the time of Jesus and beyond. Given this history of political, economic, and cultural oppression, apocalyptic spirituality no longer looked for salvation within history. If there was to be salvation of any kind, it would put an end to history altogether and bring the beginning of something new.

2. A pessimistic view of history did not mean that God's people were without a lively hope, however. In fact they looked forward to a decisive intervention by God on their behalf that would establish the kingdom of God and put an end to the history of this world in which they had suffered so much. Apocalyptic Judaism and Christianity looked forward to the time, the kairos, in which this world and its history would end and God would establish his kingdom.

3. Apocalyptic spirituality is highly dualistic. Its adherents see so much suffering in the world that they assume there must be some malevolent force behind it. God stands over against this evil force, and the history of the human race and the whole cosmos serves as the arena in which they war with one another. The apocalyptic view

makes a radical distinction between good and evil and has little room for ambiguity or gray areas. The forces of light and darkness are involved in a cosmic struggle, and there is no room for neutrality. You are either on one side or the other.

4. This struggle between good and evil will reach its climax at the end of time. At that time one final, cosmic battle will be fought in which God will conquer the forces of evil.

5. Having conquered evil, God or his agent, the Son of Man, will judge between those on the side of light and those on the side of darkness. Only those whose lives are marked by a goodness manifest in their faithfulness to God's covenant with his people will be brought into the promised kingdom of God.

6. This rewarding of the good and punishing of the evil cannot take place completely within time. Too many have suffered and died for their faith without receiving any perceptible reward in this life. Therefore, the apocalyptic outlook is marked by a belief in resurrection, in which the just will receive their due reward in a new risen life.

7. Apocalyptic literature often describes the coming of the kingdom of God in terms of a re-creation. Lacking any experience of what the end-time might be like, apocalyptic writers describe it first as an un-creation, a destruction of the order God originally created as the forces of light and darkness struggle with one another. The sun, the moon, and the stars which God placed in their appointed orbits will fall from the sky; the earth which God set firmly on it foundations will be shaken to its core. Having conquered evil in this destructive battle, God will then begin anew and re-create the heavens and the earth for God's people.

8. In some apocalyptic writings, Elijah or the Mosaic prophet of Deuteronomy 18:15 will come before this end-time struggle, announcing the coming of God and the kingdom.

9. Apocalyptic literature uses a great deal of imagery borrowed from the mythologies of the ancient Near East. It is, therefore, a highly symbolic type of literature, which loves to hide its secrets behind

an esoteric symbolic code. You have to be an initiate to understand its full meaning. Thus we find it difficult to read in our time.

Using this apocalyptic background, Mark structures his first chapter to enhance and draw out the implications of the central message he has delivered in 1:14–15 and 1:32–34. Mark begins with a compilation of prophetic quotations:

As it is written in Isaiah the prophet:
Behold, I am sending my messenger ahead of you;
He will prepare your way.

A voice of one crying out in the desert:
Prepare the way of the Lord,
Make straight his paths. (NAB)

Mark attributes these words to Isaiah, but in fact he takes them from Malachi 3:1 as well as Isaiah 40:3, with a hint of Exodus 23:20, which predicts an angelic guide for God's people. The lines from Malachi would awaken in Mark's reader an expectation of the end-time, for Malachi had prophesied that God would send his messenger before him when God came to act decisively to put an end to evil and save his faithful people. Mark takes the quotation from the book of Isaiah from the beginning of the oracles of Second Isaiah. This exilic prophet reworked and bound together two important themes of the Hebrew Scriptures: creation and the exodus. He did not emphasize the past, however, but rather the future action of God. He weaves the notions of exodus and creation together to describe the mighty acts by which God will restore his exiled people to their land and their status as his chosen people.

The line from Isaiah quoted by Mark opens a passage that combines these motifs. God will create the highway of the new exodus for the return of his people to their land. God will recreate the earth, uprooting mountains and filling in valleys to save and reconstitute his people once again. Thus with his quotations in 1:2–3, Mark has already begun to raise the apocalyptic expectations of his readers. He has us looking for the messenger who will come before God, preparing his way, and he has us thinking in terms of a new re-creative act of God that will save his people in the same way that God saved them from their slavery long ago in Egypt.

Mark then introduces John the Baptist. He so pictures John that there can be no doubt in the reader's mind that John is Elijah, the promised prophet who would come before the Lord. Mark borrows his picture of John's dress from 2 Kings 1:8, which describes the dress of Elijah. Mark quotes Malachi 3:1 to depict John as Elijah, for Malachi 4:5-6 calls the forerunner Elijah. Mark places John out in the wilderness because the wilderness is reminiscent of new beginnings: the void out of which God originally created the world and the desert in which God created his first people, Israel. Thus God's new creation and exodus begin like those of old, in the desert, in the emptiness of the wasteland. John, the herald of the new age, announces the one who will follow him and prepares the people for this new beginning with a baptism of repentance. Here in Mark, John does not announce the kingdom as he does in Matthew's gospel. In Mark that role is reserved for Jesus.

With our expectations thus raised, Jesus comes on the scene. Jesus' baptism by John opens the story of the kingdom of God. The baptism of Jesus caused great consternation in the early Christian community. It was difficult for them to explain why Jesus needed baptism by John, especially when there may have been some competition between the followers of Jesus and those of John in the early days of the church (Acts 19:1-7). The fourth gospel does not even mention the baptism. Luke reduces it to a backdrop for the descent of the Spirit upon Jesus by placing it in a subordinate clause (Lk 3:21). Matthew reports it, but feels obliged to address the question of why Jesus would need baptism. He includes a discussion between Jesus and John the Baptist regarding why Jesus' baptism is necessary for the sake of fulfillment. Only in Mark does the baptism of Jesus play an integral role in the dramatic action, for in the baptism the Father anoints Jesus to be the agent of God's kingdom: through him God decisively acts in human history. The Father does not speak to the crowds as he does in Matthew, but to Jesus, whom he is calling to a special role in the salvation of God's people. Mark has no infancy narrative or introductory poem about the incarnation. Instead, the story of our salvation begins with the call of Jesus at his baptism.

After his anointing, the Spirit drives Jesus into the wilderness, the arena of God's creative activity. In the desert Jesus struggles with Satan. To an apocalyptic mind the meaning of this desert struggle is clear. The end-time battle between the forces of light and darkness has begun. The drama of the end-time is under way. The struggle, however, is not quite what the apocalyptic seers had expected. The lights of the heavens are not falling; the earth remains firm on its foundations. No monsters appear out of the sea, as the book of Revelation depicts. This battle takes place in the human heart. One man, the Son of God, dares to face the forces of evil.

Curiously, Mark does not tell us who won. But he closely links the story of the struggle in the desert to the proclamation of the kingdom in 1:14–15. Those verses proclaim the victory of God over Satan through the faithfulness of his Son in the face of evil. Jesus wins the victory in the desert, in the void and emptiness where God's action always begins. With the defeat of Satan the kingdom of God begins to become a reality. Now the kairos, the ripe time for humanity and its hopes and dreams, is at hand.

Having made the announcement of the kingdom against this background, Mark then shows us a variety of responses and their results. The first to respond are Simon, Andrew, James, and John. These four will form the inner core of Jesus' followers, and Mark will explore the meaning of discipleship by following their responses throughout the story of Jesus. In his story of these four men, Mark works out his notion of what a faith-filled response to the proclamation of God's kingdom entails.

At this point Mark is making several key points about discipleship. To embrace the promises and hopes of the kingdom of God, the disciple must leave an old world behind. Discipleship dislodges and dislocates. The four leave their families and occupation as fishermen to follow Jesus. The change in fundamental life patterns that the kingdom calls for cuts deeply. The disciples must let old worlds die. The kingdom calls them to let go of old patterns of relating to others and change how they see the world and themselves. The gospel summons the disciples to live the pattern of hope that the dreams of the kingdom hold out. A new imagination fired by a new vision begins to shape the life of the disciples, and they begin to live differently. To have faith is to take a step on the path that this new vision has opened.

Secondly, the disciple cannot do this alone, but needs the support of others in the Christian community. An individual cannot re-create the face of the earth. However, a community moved by the Spirit and vision of Jesus can. The first disciples left the world of their nets and boats as a group, and together they followed Jesus.

Having described the challenge of discipleship, Mark shows us the results of this walking in faith by presenting his reader with the first miracle of Jesus in 1:23–28. Like Jesus' first words, the literary device of enclosure marks the story of this first mighty act of Jesus. This chiastic structure has three elements which again run A B A'. The A elements, which mention Jesus' teaching with authority, introduce and close the miracle story. A response of amazement is standard in any miracle story, but here the amazement is not at the miracle but at Jesus' teaching. The structure looks like this:

A Jesus is teaching in the synagogue with authority.

B Jesus performs the miracle and casts the evil spirit out of the man.

A' The people are amazed at the *authority* with which Jesus teaches.

Thus Mark underscores the teaching of Jesus in this miracle story. However, as happens often in this gospel, Mark does not reveal the content of Jesus' teaching. Throughout his gospel Mark will tell us that Jesus taught, and yet he will rarely reveal the content of that teaching. To learn the content of Jesus' teaching the reader must watch the passages surrounding or near the one that mentions the fact that Jesus taught. And only in an indirect way do they show us what he taught. In this story Jesus teaches that he has defeated Satan, that he has the power to cast out evil from our lives. With regard to this miracle story, we can draw two conclusions. First, we already know the content of Jesus' proclamation, for the content of the gospel was given in 1:15. The kingdom is at hand, so Jesus must have defeated Satan in the desert. Second, the content of the teaching is the miracle itself, the B element of the chiastic structure. We can see the kingdom that Jesus proclaims in graphic form through the casting out of evil from the life of this possessed man.

It is significant that this first miracle involves the casting out of a demon, whom Jesus rebukes with authority and then sends on its way. The struggle that began in the desert in 1:12–13 continues here, but Mark makes clear who has the upper hand. Jesus is defeating Satan in the great battle of the end-time. However, Mark reinterprets the apocalyptic tradition here. The battle is not fought throughout the cosmos with the sun, moon, and stars falling from the sky. The battle is of cosmic proportions, but it takes place within the human heart. God's re-creation not only involves a new heaven and earth, but first and foremost it re-creates the landscape of the human spirit and makes human life whole.

Finally, with regard to this first miracle, the text raises the question of Jesus' identity for the first time. The demon knows who Jesus is, but Jesus quickly silences him. The crowds are left in amazement. The question of the identity of Jesus will continue to be an issue in this gospel. Why Jesus seems to hide his identity is not yet apparent. We will have to wait for more evidence in later chapters to address it.

Mark continues with miracle stories to show us how God reshapes the human landscape through the work of his Son, Jesus. Jesus next encounters Peter's mother-in-law, who is suffering with a fever. Jesus simply takes her by the hand and helps her rise. It is a very short story, but it has three important themes that are worth the reader's attention. First, Jesus performs this second miracle for the sake of a woman. Throughout the gospel Mark tries to balance male and female when he shows how the power of the kingdom of God is at work. In the kingdom of God distinctions made on the basis of gender are not valid. God works equally through all, in all, and for all. Secondly, Jesus helps the woman rise. The quiet reference to the resurrection, where the promises of the kingdom will be fully realized, is no accident. Through her healing, which restores her to wholeness, the woman experiences a small foretaste of the resurrection. Finally, Peter's mother-in-law rises and begins to serve others. Again, we have a very quick phrase that alludes to a major theme of discipleship in this gospel. The disciple serves. To enter into the kingdom and to embrace its dreams means to serve. Later Mark will expand and further explore this theme of service, for it is one of the keys to the mystery of the kingdom. For now, we simply see that someone touched by the promises of the kingdom begins to use the life that they have been given for the sake of service to others.

Having shown us these two miracles, Mark now moves to his summary statement in 1:32–34. This summary takes these first two miracles and tells us that things like this were happening in great numbers. Mark wants his readers to note how widely the conflict between the kingdoms of God and Satan rages, and how great the victory of God is. He pictures Jesus' ministry in Galilee as a triumphant march (*parousia*) in which the kingdom of God touches numerous lives and transforms them. In Isaiah 40 the prophet's vision of the victorious march of God in a new exodus emphasized God's re-creating the physical earth for the sake of his people; Mark, on the other hand, sees Galilee flowering with the results of God's re-creation of human life. Mark continues to locate the eschatological action of God within the human realm. He also stresses the widespread success of Jesus' proclamation. In 1:37 Simon tells Jesus that everyone is looking for him. It is a way of saying, "the whole world has been waiting for this." Human dreams from time immemorial come to fruition in the work of Jesus. Jesus responds by moving out to other towns so that the re-creative march of God's kingdom may spread further.

The chapter closes with another detailed miracle story in which Jesus cures a leper. The leper not only has a physical disability because of his disease, he also has spiritual, communal, and personal problems. Leprosy marred a person physically with skin sores; it also made him or her ritually unclean and communally untouchable. Lepers were forced to live outside of human settlements, often in cemeteries, away from family and friends. Because of this ritually imposed exile, they were to some extent already dead socially. Leprosy also was a sign of one's alienation from God. The people of Jesus' time had no good medical explanation for this disease. They saw it as a result of the anger of God at some sin the victim must have committed. As a punishment, leprosy made the victim ritually unclean and hence unfit for temple worship. Finally, the disease must have destroyed a person's self-image. Rejected by God, excluded from their community, required to wear a bell to warn people away, the leper's self-esteem must have been very low. Imagine trying to walk around downtown in any of our cities ringing a bell and crying out for people to stay away because you had a dreaded disease. After a few hours of seeing yourself reflected in the fearful eyes of others, your image of yourself would quickly turn negative, and you might wish you could exist far from the community of others.

The healing of this leper restores not only the man's health but also his relationship with God, makes him welcome again in the community, and helps him see himself as valued and loved by God. Closing this first section of the gospel, the story of the leper shows that the kingdom of God re-creates human life in all of its dimensions. This gospel contains many miracle stories, most of them about the healing of bodies. From the very first, Mark tells us to look not only at the physical dimension of healing, but also at the re-creation and making whole of all the dimensions of human life. This miracle also repeats several of the themes we have already seen. Jesus' authority is reaffirmed ("If you will to do so, you can cure me"). Jesus overcomes the evil that plagues human life and has trapped us in the present impasse. And the secretiveness of Jesus about his identity appears again ("see that you tell no one anything"). The story closes with Mark's emphasizing that the effects and message of the kingdom are becoming so well known that Jesus can no longer move about publicly. The last word in this opening movement of the gospel is that of the kingdom's immeasurable success in Galilee.

Reflections in Front of the Text

The world in which we live is not simply an objective reality that stands hard and fast over against human experience. It is not merely the sum of all things that exist, a cosmic environment for human life. Our world is an interpreted reality. Human beings transcend every possible environment and create for themselves worlds of meaning through which they integrate all that they encounter into a meaningful whole. The world of the Greek city-state with its participative forms of civic life differed greatly from the world of the ancient Near Eastern despotism of the Persian Empire.

The world of eleventh-century Europe, dominated by feudal lords and monasteries, was a very different time and place from the world of the twentieth-century, which was dominated by a technological imagination and corporate interests. The worlds in which human life takes place are correlative realities. The things that catch our attention mirror the questions humans deem worth asking; the things we value reflect what reality reveals of itself to us in a particular world. The ancient Greeks sought a principle of unity and explanation beneath the manifoldness of life, and they became philosophers. The Romans asked how they could manage their physical and social environment, and in doing so they became great engineers and legislators. People living in the eleventh-century looked at the world symbolically and asked how the things that filled their lives spoke of something more, the things of God. They became monks and nuns and theologians.

Imagination and images structure our worlds. Our imaginations free us from a simple stimulus-response relationship to the environment so that we begin to ask what reality means and what is possible for human life. Certain images become key to the worlds we construct. They shape our perception and understanding. They guide our anticipations and longings. They forge our desires and wills. Examples abound in contemporary culture. After September 11, 2001, the American flag took on greater significance than before to the people of the United States. It spoke to us of our unity as a people in the face of the attack on our homeland, and it became a symbol of our resolve to seek justice and ensure the security of our people. Advertising abounds with symbols. An advertisement for an automobile does not just tell us about the car. It tells us what we can become if we own it. It shapes our desires. The picture of an astronaut standing on the surface of the moon speaks to us of our technological achievements and calls us to further exploration of the universe.

Mark's first box containing the mystery of the kingdom quickly attracts the eye. It is brightly painted and its themes of hope appeal to the reader. In this first section of his gospel Mark invites us into a different world of meaning than the one we now know. He engages our imaginations so that we might see reality differently and new possibilities in life might emerge. He reshapes our perception and understanding and guides our longings into new paths. He wants us to dream with the prophets of old. He offers us hope. The central symbol of this new world is the kingdom of God. In the stories he tells us of Jesus, Mark offers us images of that new world that can fire our imaginations.

Hope is made possible by the imagination, which sees things that are not yet realized and reaches for them. This first section of Mark's gospel seeks to awaken hope and shape the imaginations of God's people. To do this Mark always keeps an eye on the proclamation of the kingdom of God in 1:14–15. This is the heart of the matter. The task of the gospel is to call people to hope. Given the fact that Mark sees the kingdom as already impinging on the world, he does not proclaim some far distant future hope. The kingdom is possible now because God is at work in his Son Jesus now. Mark has a proleptic view of the kingdom. Its fullness may lie in the future, but its power and its possibilities are with us even now.

For Mark the end of time and the closing of this world's history were very near. Two thousand years later we have a different perspective on time. The end may not be as near as some early Christians thought. But the creative tension between the end-time and the present is alive even now with possibilities. For example, in the midst of a world of conflict that has its roots in the great inequalities of our social and economic lives, the kingdom offers a vision of justice rooted in respect for the dignity of every human individual realized in community. Jesus does not brush off anyone because his status has already been defined by the prejudices of his time. He treats the leper with respect. That respect in itself is healing. Jesus does not simply dismiss the man possessed by evil because those around him have already classified him as a sinner. So too we can find the courage to face the prejudices of our society that so often write off people because of their economic status, their gender, or their race. We can look for the good in those whose sins may have harmed us, and find room for forgiveness. We can look for economic opportunities for those who are seen as losers in the great game of capitalism. The world can be a very different place if God is at work in it through his son, Jesus.

Secondly, Mark depicts the kingdom as already transforming people's lives through exorcisms and healing. At first glance these are not everyday occurrences in our churches. Exorcism seems to have become the domain of Hollywood, and Christian congregations rarely feel the need for an exorcism, much less actually experience one. But they do struggle with evil in their own hearts and in the world in which they work, play and enjoy their lives. Sin is both individual and social. It warps and distorts the heart of each person, and it corrupts and perverts the lives of institutions great and small. Sin is both a question of particular acts and a matter of basic attitudes and fundamental patterns out of which individual acts emerge.

Sin and evil can possess us. One can see this in two fundamental flaws of our society—its excessive individualism and its consumerism. These two fundamental habits of the heart shape our lives as individuals as well as the fundamental patterns of our corporations and our government's decisions. They define how we see the world and what is possible and desirable in life. The gospel gives us the power of hope so that we can name the evil that comes from excessive individualism and consumerism. The gospel helps us recognize that Christ has already conquered these evils and that a better world is possible.

Thus the proclamation of the kingdom as the conquest of Satan and evil is a message of great hope. Jesus has defeated what seems to possess us and trap us in patterns that destroy life. We are free. The gospel proclaims that we are caught up in a new Exodus, a re-creation of the human landscape. The power of God at work in Jesus, conquering evil, provides the key to the story of Jesus' wrestling with Satan in the desert, and it also stands out in the first miracle of Jesus in which he simply assumes command of the evil spirit and tells it to be gone. Jesus has won the victory over evil, and he controls the field of battle. The preacher and the reader of the gospel have a great opportunity to name the evils we struggle with and echo the words of Jesus, "Be gone."

The Christian community does not experience dramatic physical healings as part of the everyday stuff of our lives. But healing should be central to our Christian experience. The kingdom of God promises us wholeness of life. Mark paints a much broader picture of the healing work of Jesus than what we see in its most dramatic occurrences. Healing involves more than the physical and the individual. The healing of the leper, which Mark places in the key position as the final story of this section, invites us to consider how healing can also touch our social relationships, our relationship with God, and even our fundamental sense of ourselves. Healing always restores us to the community that is the kingdom of God.

Third, hope is not wishful thinking. The call for change and trust in the good news summons us to conversion today. That conversion is not simply a matter of beliefs that we hold to be true or a change in how we act. It means changing our way of being in the world. It involves a profound shift in how we see the world and what is possible in life. It affects how we understand ourselves, our relationships, the institutions within which we carry out our lives, and the basic patterns that structure our lives. It alters our sense of ourselves and of what it means to be human.

It changes the images we use to understand God. God, who approaches us out of the future, re-creates, heals, and delivers us from evil.

Key Points for Preaching

This section of Mark's gospel calls preachers to awaken hope in their hearers and reshape the imaginations of God's people. In doing so, they are wise never to lose sight of the central proclamation of this section of the gospel and the gospel as a whole in 1:14–15. The kingdom of God is at hand. Its dreams are possible. Every story in this section of the gospel in one way or another draws out the implications of that centerpiece. The homilist has the wonderful opportunity to invite people to dream and live the possibilities of those dreams. For "we are such stuff as dreams are made on" (William Shakespeare, *The Tempest*, IV,i.).

This first section of Mark gives the homilist the chance to reflect on the power of God present in the community in the work of Jesus. A new creation and a new exodus are taking place. We are free and God is at work recreating the landscape of human life. With the power of Jesus who has conquered Satan in the desert the homilist can invite the community to name the evils that plague God's people and command them to be gone. The community can enter the struggle to leave an old world behind and live in the light of the promises of something new. The power of God at work in the kingdom can make all aspects of our lives whole. Mark's gospel has many healing stories. All of them are more than just physical. All of them bear the promise of this multi-dimensional healing. So too the power of God can heal our relationships, our sense of our selves, and our relationship with God beyond our wildest imagination.

In reflecting on this section of Mark, the homilist has the opportunity to picture a world shaped by the future that God holds out to us and ask what it means to live as if that future were truly possible. How would we live if justice for all people really could be attained and if God had created the world so that there are enough goods that all may live well? How would we live if forgiveness were really possible? How would I see myself if God sees a goodness within that is worth healing? How would we deal with our hurts and disappointments if forgiveness can heal our relationships? What does it mean to live as if peace were possible in the world and in our hearts? Preaching the first section of Mark opens a world of possibilities to the congregation.

Finally, Mark's concern to overcome gender and racial bias ought to mark our preaching. In this first section Mark carefully balances the stories of the realization of God's promises for a man and a woman. Later in the third chapter the list of regions from which people come to hear Jesus and to be touched by the power of God at work through him includes Jewish as well as Gentile lands. As far as Mark is concerned, the kingdom does not discriminate in any way on the basis of race or gender. The world our homilies envision ought not to be touched by such biases either. Our language ought to be inclusive. Sexism and racism ought to be among those social patterns of sin that we proclaim Jesus has conquered.

CHAPTER TWO

CONFRONTATIONS

Mark 2:1–3:6

Stop dwelling on past events
And brooding over days gone by.
I am about to do something new;
This moment it will unfold.
Can you not perceive it?

Isaiah 43:18–19 (Revised English Bible)

The World of the Text

It is one thing to hope and dream, to live in the light of the promises
God has made and watch the power of God re-create the human world.
It is another to embrace that dream and walk the path that it offers. The
first of the many layered boxes that contain the secret of the gospel is
quite an attractive reality. But Mark nudges us and beckons us to open
it and look at what lies inside. Another box, another layer in the mystery of the kingdom of God, reveals a further step on the path where
Jesus leads. This new box pictures conflict erupting in the midst of the
dreams of the kingdom.

The second movement of the gospel runs from 2:1 to 3:6. Each story
in it pictures Jesus and the kingdom he proclaims meeting resistance.

He is opposed when he assumes the authority to forgive sins, is questioned about the company he keeps, challenged to live according to the norms of the Pharisees and John's disciples, and confronted over his power to set aside the Sabbath laws regarding picking grain and healing. The real issues at the heart of the controversies lie deeper, however. They have to do with different images of God that underlie the opposing positions taken by Jesus and his adversaries. They also concern how God works in human history: is God's work encapsulated in established religious traditions as the opponents of Jesus think, or does God break into human history and upset even traditions that are rooted in God's earlier deeds?

Not surprisingly, Mark structures this second movement of the gospel chiastically. The pattern is A B C B′ A′. In both of the A stories Mark takes a simple miracle account and expands it to include a confrontational dialogue. Thus he transforms these miracle stories into accounts of conflict. Both of the B stories involve food. They concern the company Jesus is keeping at table and the question of whether it is permissible to pick grain on the Sabbath. The central C story confronts the issue of fasting and contains the mysterious words about not putting new wine into old wineskins. The structure provides the key in that everything points to the C story at the center. All the confrontations have something to do with not putting new wine into old wineskins.

The first A story narrates the cure of the paralytic in 2:1–12. It bears the threefold structure of any good miracle story: it presents the problem; it shows Jesus resolving the problem; and it tells about the reaction of the crowd to what has occurred. In this story, however, Mark breaks open the structure of the miracle form to include the element of controversy in 2:6–11. Two results follow. First, Mark begins to demonstrate that the miracles that result from faith in the kingdom occasion opposition on the part of some that is deeply rooted. For as we have seen, the miracles of the kingdom are more than just physical. As with the healing of the leper in chapter one, they have physical, communal, and religious implications. They tell us how God acts and for whom God cares. In this second movement of the gospel, opposition develops against the image of God that Jesus makes known in his actions, an image in which mercy and forgiveness take precedence over strict observance of the Law.

The Jewish authorities oppose not so much the physical healing as Jesus' presuming to have the authority to forgive sins.

Secondly, Mark's breaking open the miracle account with a conflict story deliberately confuses the forgiveness of sins with the healing of the man's paralysis. Jesus does not address the man's paralysis, but proclaims that the paralytic's sins are forgiven. This fusion of forgiveness and healing raises questions in the minds of the scribes about the source of Jesus' authority, for no human has the power to forgive sins. Jesus settles the dispute by healing the paralytic's physical ailment, thus demonstrating his power to forgive sin. This deliberate merging of the power to forgive with the power to heal forces the reader to recognize that Jesus' miracles have more than one dimension. To forgive is to heal and to heal is to forgive. Mark is commenting not only on this particular miracle, but also on all the miracles in his gospel. He calls the reader to recognize the many dimensions that the kingdom of God touches in our lives, and he shows that there is resistance in history to that kind of healing and to the image of a God who so indiscriminately bestows the benefits of his kingdom.

Finally, the action in this story takes place in the context of Jesus preaching. Again Mark pictures Jesus proclaiming God's word but does not tell the reader what Jesus was saying. The actions of Jesus contain his teaching.

We move next to the first of the B stories, both of which deal with food. The first of these runs from 2:13 to 2:17 and involves the call of Levi and the discussion around the fact that Jesus is eating with sinners. Again the passage mentions the fact that Jesus taught but tells us nothing of what he says. We must watch Jesus in action to get his message. The teaching lies in the fact that Jesus, acting in the name of God, is willing to sit down at table with sinners. Jesus' action proclaims the gospel news that sinners are welcome at the banquet of the kingdom.

Two issues dominate this story. The first has to do with status or dignity. Jewish society looked down upon both Levi, the tax collector, and the sinners with whom Jesus shares table fellowship. Although he may be rich, Levi is unacceptable because he cooperates with the Roman occupation forces by collecting taxes for them from the Jewish people. The sinners are unacceptable because they have broken the Torah, the

Law. Both have betrayed their Jewish heritage by breaking their covenant with God and his people. Levi and the sinners, then, are social outcasts. Jesus, however, does not operate on that presupposition. He accepts these people, and treats them with dignity by sharing his company with them. His actions announce that he does not share the opinion of the religious authorities, who see these people as religious rejects. To his critics Jesus appears to be throwing God's pearls before swine. However, he himself does not see sinners and tax collectors as swine, nor does God. He grants them their human dignity and treats them as if they had value in God's eyes. Jesus' religious judgment is then at odds with the social and religious wisdom of his time. A more important issue underlies this incident, however. Jesus' religious judgment about the status of these people in the eyes of God demonstrates something of God's own attitude and action. Just as Jesus' notion of God and God's purposes differs from that of the religious leaders of his time, Jesus' actions raise serious questions about the nature and attitude of God and as to whom the kingdom is offered.

The other B story, 2:23–28, again deals with food. This time the controversy centers on Jesus' disciples picking grain on the Sabbath, something the Law forbids. In Mark's account of this incident, the disciples are picking the grain for no good reason. Matthew, who seeks to preserve the Law in a Christian context, cannot let this stand, and so in 12:1 of his gospel he adds that the disciples did so because they were hungry. Having provided an appropriate motivation for setting the Law aside, Matthew also provides an interpretive principle to be applied to the Torah by quoting Hosea 6:6: what God wants is mercy, not sacrifice. Matthew's changes make this story an example of how to interpret the Torah properly in extenuating circumstances. He preserves the tremendous respect for Jewish tradition that is so central to his gospel and yet shows his community how to interpret that tradition in the light of what has been revealed by Jesus. He also closes the story with a simple declaration that Jesus is the master of the Sabbath and can do as he pleases.

Mark does not have the same respect for the tradition and, in fact, includes this story to challenge the tradition directly. In Mark's version the disciples pick the grain for no stated reason and with no justification. Thus Mark asks not how to preserve, yet interpret, Torah, but whether the Torah has validity any longer. Mark closes the story not only with Jesus' saying the Son of Man is master of the Sabbath, but also with Jesus stating that the Sabbath is subordinate to human concerns. The Sabbath is made for human beings; human beings were not made so they could keep the Sabbath. Sabbath and Law are subject to something greater that has come on the scene with Jesus, the kingdom of God. Nothing, not even traditions that have been given by God to his people in the past, can get in the way of what God is doing now through Jesus. Once again Mark raises questions about what it is that God is up to here. Whatever God is doing through Jesus, it cannot be made to fit old patterns or pat conceptions of how God works. Something new is breaking into human history, and it does not fit old moulds.

The second A story, 3:1–6, resembles the first in that Mark breaks a miracle story open to include a confrontational dialogue. Just as in the story of the picking of grain on the Sabbath, this passage depicts Jesus setting aside the Sabbath law in the light of something more important, the breaking in of the kingdom. Again Jesus confronts the religious leaders of his people. The argument involves not just the healing of one man's withered hand, but the primacy of either the Torah or the kingdom, the old or the new. Also at issue is the appropriate understanding of God and of God's purposes in human life. It is ironic that the healing, which the Pharisees see as breaking the Sabbath law, enables the man with the withered hand to partake in the Sabbath. God created the Sabbath so that human beings might enjoy creation with God and praise God for his goodness. Jesus has healed this man in an act of eschatological re-creation so that he might now join fully with God in the Sabbath celebration. The Pharisees are so bound by their limited vision of how God acts that they cannot see that what Jesus is doing actually enhances the Sabbath they seek to protect.

Given the chiastic structure of this section, A B C B′ A′, the central C story in 2:18–22 provides the key to interpreting the whole section. The discussion centers on the fact that Jesus and his disciples do not abide by the common fasting practices of the Pharisees and John the Baptist's disciples. Jesus deals with the issue by stating that one does not fast when the bridegroom has arrived. The bridegroom symbolizes the arrival of the kingdom, so that Jesus in fact says that the kingdom has arrived and that the religious response to it does not fit the old patterns of interacting with God that people are used to. There then follow the key lines of this whole section of the gospel: you don't put a new patch on an old cloak or new wine in old wineskins. The newness of the kingdom does not suit old patterns of religious practice. The kingdom calls for something new: new ways of thinking about God and how God acts in our lives, new ways of responding to the work of God in creation, and new ways of interacting with one another.

Chapter 2:20 presents a problem, for it says there will come a time when the bridegroom is taken and then his disciples will fast. This statement does not fit the context of the story or this section of the gospel. Some scholars believe it is an interpolation, something added to the gospel by a later editor who was guiding Christian ascetic practices at a time when the kingdom did not prove to be as imminent as it was first thought to be. Others think Mark included the statement to guide his Christian community to the new practice of fasting on Friday, the day the bridegroom was taken from them.

Each of the stories in this section places the newness of the kingdom in confrontation with old religious notions and practices. It forces the reader to ask what kind of God we have who forgives those who were previously thought to be religious outcasts, who re-creates human life and does not let the traditions and the Torah stand in his way, who places the human above the tradition. It forces the reader to ask many questions: who is religiously and socially acceptable? What patterns of inclusion and exclusion rule our lives? Do we have room in our lives for God to move in new ways? Have our religious practices so boxed in God in that God cannot move in new ways?

The central theme of this section of the gospel, then, is confrontation over several important issues. The stories of this second section of the gospel challenge traditional views of God and how God acts in human life. They question exactly what God is doing in our lives. They open a debate over the relationship of the old and the new, the tradition and the kingdom. The conflict over these issues takes place on several levels. The obvious level is the conflict between Jesus and his opponents. We are already given intimations of where this conflict will end by 3:6: they are already plotting Jesus' demise.

A second level of conflict may have been taking place within the Markan community. Such matters as the role of the Torah in the Christian community, who is acceptable at table fellowship, and whether and when Christians ought to fast may have split that community. In the midst of such disputes Mark makes his position clear. The kingdom takes precedence over all other considerations. The prime consideration in the discussion of all these issues ought to be openness to God's doing something new in our lives. Mark takes a liberal stand very close to that of Paul on the matter of the Law. Matthew, on the other hand, takes the traditionalist position. He is open to the new, but the old is kept as well. For Matthew, the new brings fulfillment to things that have been in place for centuries. Matthew changes the Markan saying to read, "Neither is new wine put into old wineskins; otherwise the skins burst, and wine is spilled and the skins are destroyed; but new wine is put into fresh wineskins, and so both are preserved" (Mt 9:17 NRSV). Mark does not worry about preserving both the old and the new. The issue at hand is whether we will move into the new world of the kingdom of God, not wondering what we can take with us of the old world.

Reflections in Front of the Text

This section of the gospel opens yet a third arena of conflict, the difficult one found in the life of the reader of the gospel. Paul Tillich, the great Lutheran theologian of the twentieth century, dealt with the theme of creativity and the new under the rubric of the polarity of dynamics and form. Dynamics for Tillich involves pure energy, a life force, the potential to become. We cannot easily name it, for, once named, it has taken on form, its polar opposite. We never have dynamics in its purity, but we know when we come close to its pure state. It is the toddler loose in the kitchen, exploring the cupboards within his reach and dispersing the elements of a well-ordered kitchen all over the floor. It is the hurricane or the tornado that wreaks havoc along its path. It is the chaos of the watery abyss over which the Spirit of God hovered before the creation. While dynamics has immense potential for creativity, it also holds the possibility of destruction, for when uncontrolled it becomes chaos.

Form, on the other hand, provides structure. It is that which defines, brings about harmony, and sets boundaries. It is the essence of things that are, which allows beings an ordered existence. Form brings order to the energy of chaos.

The trick with dynamics and form, as with any of Tillich's polarities, is not to see them as opposites struggling with one another, but as two elements which need one another and which participate in each other. They orbit one another like double stars whose gravity has them locked in a common celestial dance. When form and dynamics come together, the dance is something beautiful to behold. They mutually enhance one another in a work of art that gives perfect expression to its subject. When form and dynamics slip away from one another, two very dangerous tendencies appear. On the one hand, a strict formalism can squeeze the life out of anything. It can happen in art, when the canons of what is acceptable are not open to innovation and new expressions of the beautiful. It can happen to institutions that have fallen out of touch with the human purposes they are meant to serve. It occurs in a liturgy that has become nothing more than a dry following of the rubrics and does not touch the life of the congregation. On the other hand, dynamics set loose on its own becomes chaotic and destructive, never able to bring the energy at its core to a creative expression. It is revolution and change simply for the sake of revolution and change.

The problem with change and creativity is that for the new to be born, old forms must be left behind. When an individual or a people set out on a journey to a new world, they must leave the old world that was familiar to them. For a while they must stand in the midst of a creative chaos between ordered worlds, the old and the new. The Scriptures understand this polarity and play on it a great deal. The primary images they use for chaos are watery storms and desert wastelands. Thus God must face the watery chaos before speaking, and begin to bring form to the vital energy present in the creation story of Genesis. When the human race oversteps the boundaries of the created order through sin, the world disintegrates into watery chaos in the flood of Noah's days. The people of Israel must pass through the watery chaos of the Red Sea and the sojourn in the desert as they pass from a world of slavery in Egypt to the world of the Promised Land. In this journey God creates them as a people. When Job's life disintegrates around him, he faces chaos not only in the circumstances of his life, but also in his heart as he struggles to find some reason that will make sense out of his dilemma. God finally appears to him out of the watery chaos of the storm in Job 38.

In the first section of his gospel Mark has asked us to leave an old world behind and live in the light of the possibilities of the kingdom of God. It is no accident that God begins the creation of this new world of the kingdom in the wasteland of 1:12, where a life and death struggle with evil is fought before the new can be born. God creates out of chaos once again. Mark has invited us to a new world that comes into being as God acts in human life through his Son, Jesus. There is a problem, however. As one very well-ordered world is left behind and before the other comes clearly into view, we must live in the chaos of the transition. That chaos can inspire fear and invite reaction. Mark wants us to pray over that fear and that negative reaction as we contemplate the clues to the secret of the kingdom contained in this second layer of his gospel.

Mark would have us look at the patterns in our own lives that resist the promises of the kingdom. What in our lives do we not want to let go of so that re-creation can take place and something new can come to be? The first box containing the mystery of the kingdom makes the promises and power of the kingdom look inviting. This second box forces us to look at what it is in our lives that resists the promises of God. What securities must we let go of? What fears dominate our attitudes and actions? What patterns of sin close us to what God is doing in our world?

A world of meaning is a comprehensive interpretation of human experience. It explains reality to those who live within its understanding and shows its participants what is possible for human action. It is a way of being in the world. Certain key elements make up any such world of meaning. It must explain the physical world in which we live both on the grand scale of cosmology and on the far more practical level of everyday life. It must be able to tell us how and why the planets and stars move in the heavens and also be able to warn us that fire can burn and that falls from great heights can be dangerous. Next, a world must give us a sense of the social realities that shape our lives. These would include how great institutions such as education, law, government, and religion function. On a simpler level they give us a sense of what it means to be a father, a mother, a leader. They help us make sense of our sexuality and gender roles. Out of all this, a world gives us a basic sense of ourselves and what it means to be human. It tells us how we fit into the physical and social worlds, what our appropriate roles are, and what possibilities life holds. Our sense of self is deeply intertwined with our sense of our social and physical worlds. Finally, our world gives us a sense of our God. Our fundamental images for our God emerge out of our sense of the physical and social worlds.

All of these elements are sources of resistance to the new world the gospel asks us to imagine. If the justice and peace the kingdom promises are to reign in human life, institutions of government, law, economics, and education must undergo profound changes. Our fundamental sense of ourselves must shift. We must re-imagine what our lives are about, and the possibilities we see in life must shift. New images of God emerge in the kingdom. God no longer simply guarantees the religious institutions of the past. The God of Jesus, his Father, must become the center of our lives. We get a glimpse of the nature of God when Jesus sits down at table with sinners, offers forgiveness beyond our wildest dreams, takes care of human needs in spite of the laws of the Sabbath, and heals so that we might enjoy creation with God on the Sabbath. Religion that centers on the self or on the power of those who rule its institutions must give way. Even our orientation in time must change. A past order that God constituted and continues to guarantee no longer determines our lives, but rather, a God who approaches us out of the future shapes the promises that life holds.

All this is threatening. We do not have to take many steps down the path of this conversion to sense the chaos that might envelop us as we leave one comfortable world for another that God holds out to us. The chaos within our hearts and minds threatens even more than external circumstances, as we venture into a promised land that is not the familiar world we have known. Mark wants us to listen for whatever makes us hesitate, whatever holds us back, whatever shouts no. If we do not face it, we cannot move into the kingdom that has been promised.

In baptism we all passed through the waters of chaos. We left an old world and an old self, and we entered a new creation. This conversion is a lifelong journey, and there are times when the change baptism calls for is too much and the possible chaos too threatening and overwhelming.

In these Markan passages Jesus and his notions of the kingdom and the God who offers us the kingdom become too threatening for some institutions; they are too much for some individuals, even some of those who have chosen to be his followers. Mark invites us to come to terms with the chaos, and with the fears and hesitations it engenders. It is wonderful to dream and hope. It is difficult to wake up, face the conflict, and walk the path to the world our hopes hold out to us.

Key Points for Preaching

Once again the preacher must rivet his attention on the central passage of this section of the gospel. The notion that we cannot put new wine in old wineskins shapes every story in this second section of Mark. It calls us to take a hard look at the conflicts the gospel can introduce into our lives.

Perhaps the greatest gift the homilist can give the congregation in preaching on this section is the insight that the gospel causes conflict. We can then go on to help name what the conflicts might be in our own lives. Those conflicts will be internal struggles of the soul as we wrestle with our fears and doubts. It is difficult to let go of one way of understanding the world and embrace another. But the struggles will also be social. For if the gospel is to take root, not only must individuals change, but also the ways in which we structure our society. Good preaching will recognize that the gospel challenges our deepest values and beliefs. Even the way we know and understand God and what God is up to in our lives must undergo radical change. Conversion runs that deep.

The homilist must recognize that such great changes can engender chaos in the minds and hearts of individuals and within society. Martin Luther King heard the call of the gospel. His proclamation of it called forth violent reactions on the part of some; it changed the laws and way of life of the land; and it led to his death. A good homily can help people chart a course out of slavery through the waters of chaos so that they can become a new people on the far side of the turbulence.

Finally, in dealing with this section of the gospel, the preacher must not lose sight of the themes of the first section. We can face the chaos and the conflict because we have seen and experienced the promises of the kingdom. We know that it is the power of God that is at work in our midst. So anything is possible for those who have faith.

CHAPTER THREE

DECISIONS

Mark: 3:7–35

I shall be telling this with a sigh
Somewhere ages and ages hence;
Two roads diverged in a wood, and I
I took the one less traveled by,
And that has made all the difference.

Robert Frost, "The Road Not Taken"

The World of the Text

In Robert Frost's poem the road not taken was "just as fair," but that is not so in the gospel of Mark. The paths that stand before us in the gospel offer us the ways to two very different worlds. Far more apt for the decisions set before us in this section of the gospel are the prophetic words of Moses in the Book of Deuteronomy, "I have set before you life and death, blessings and curses. Choose life so that you and your descendants may live" (Deuteronomy 30:19, NRSV).

In our last chapter the second of Mark's boxes within boxes presented the worlds that tug at our hearts and imaginations and asked us to deal with the confrontation the gospel causes in our lives and in our society. Mark does not want us to get stuck at that point of the mystery, however. He urges us to look beyond that box with all its controversy and move on to the third box that it contains. A sign of freedom marks this next box, which is found in 3:7–35. This section summons us to choose one path or the other, one world of possibilities or its opposite. Robert Frost is right; the choice will make all the difference.

Mark structures this section in the same way as the last one. It is a five-part chiastic structure that runs A B C B′ A′. The structure allows us to look at various responses to the gospel and to see if they find echoes in our own lives. The A passages deal with those who have chosen to follow Jesus. The B and C passages show those who opt for the other road, the road of the social and religious world we know and are comfortable with. These B and C passages form an interior chiastic structure in which the B stories tell of the negative response of Jesus' family and the C passage narrates the accusations of the religious scribes in defense of their world. Thus the overall structure of the section looks like this

A The true family of Jesus: the positive response of the crowds and of the twelve.

B The negative response of Jesus' physical family who think he is mad.

C The sin against the Holy Spirit: the negative response of the scribes who think Jesus is evil, a representative of Satan.

B′ Jesus' physical families try to reach him.

A′ Jesus states that his true family is made up of those who do the will of God.

At the center of the whole structure sits another of those mysterious gospel sayings we all have heard but struggle to understand: the unforgivable sin against the Holy Spirit.

The first A element, 3:7–19, shows us two positive responses to Jesus and the message of the kingdom. The first positive response in 3:7–12 echoes the Markan summary found in 1:32–34. It takes us back to the atmosphere of the first chapter with its re-creation of human life through faith in the promises of the kingdom and the overwhelmingly positive response many people have given the kingdom. Here in chapter three we find another Markan summary that emphasizes these same themes.

There are some further nuances, however. The crowds expand to include Gentiles as well as Jews. Transjordan, Tyre and Sidon all lie in Gentile territory. This inclusion of the Gentiles raises some serious theological and pastoral questions: can Gentiles share in the promises God has made to his chosen people? And if so, what kind of God is it that Jesus proclaims, a God who accepts those who were once thought to be outsiders? A God who allows other peoples to share in the inheritance he has promised his own people was not a popular idea in Jesus' time.

The response to the kingdom has become so great that the crowds are becoming unmanageable and even something of a threat to Jesus. Mark points to the great following of Jesus to demonstrate how widespread and deep this hunger for the kingdom runs in the human heart. Word is spreading rapidly of the new world God offers his people through the ministry of his Son, and people are traveling from foreign lands to hear of it and be touched by its power.

This Markan summary refers to three other key themes of the gospel that Mark will develop in more detail later. The first repeats a theme from the first chapter. Mark again draws our attention to the great number of healings taking place. The power of the kingdom continues to conquer evil and suffering and to re-create human life. Secondly, Jesus continues to silence the evil spirits lest they reveal his identity. Finally, Mark introduces the image of the boat, which will later play a prominent theological role in the gospel, for it will tie together the Jewish and Gentile sides of the Sea of Galilee. Let us just note for now that the boat appears when the gospel gives us the first glimpse of the Gentile question.

The first A element of the section's structure then tightens its focus. Chapter 3:7–12 show us vast crowds of Jews and Gentiles coming to Jesus. The second part of the A element, 3:13–19, illustrates the positive response to Jesus in greater detail by looking closely at the Twelve. It too picks up themes already developed in the first chapter. In 1:16–20, the first story after the announcement of the kingdom in 1:14–15, the first four disciples left their families and their occupations to follow Jesus. That story emphasized how the kingdom calls for a radical change in one's life. The kingdom uproots these four men from their former lives and leads them on new paths.

In chapter three Mark expands this inner core to the Twelve. If chapter one emphasized how the kingdom called them out of their old way of life, chapter three shows us what the Twelve embrace. Mark calls them companions of Jesus and tells us they shared the mission of Jesus from the very beginning. Jesus sends them to preach the kingdom and gives them power to cast out demons. Their work, like that of Jesus, is one of re-creating human life. The Twelve will play a crucial role in the gospel. Mark has already shown us how great was the response to Jesus' message of the kingdom, but he wants to focus the attention of his reader on exactly what this response entails. The Twelve serve as close-up studies of what discipleship means. Mark gives us an early hint about where all this will lead: in 3:19 he says that Jesus will be betrayed by one of the Twelve. The Twelve have hardly begun to share the mission of Jesus when the shadow of their failure already looms on the horizon.

After showing us the enthusiastic response of the crowds to the message of the kingdom and then focusing our attention on the Twelve as the paradigm of what discipleship means, Mark immediately contrasts these two groups with two groups who respond negatively, the scribes and the family of Jesus. Mark ties these two groups closely together in the B and C elements of the chiastic structure: he surrounds the account of the argument with the scribes with two accounts of the lack of faith on the part of Jesus' family. In this way the two examples of a negative response to Jesus and the kingdom reinforce and comment on one another.

The first B element, the response of Jesus' family, is found in 3:20-21. His family is reacting to two things. The response to Jesus has become so overwhelming that the whole matter is getting out of hand; they cannot even find the space and time to have a meal together. Beyond that, they think Jesus is out of his mind and want to get the whole affair back under control by taking charge of him. The newness of the kingdom so disrupts their comfortable established patterns of life that it must be insane, and in all charity they must now take care of Jesus and get things back to normal. Mark hits upon a key theme of these opening chapters once again. The kingdom is new and does not fit old patterns. One response to it is to simply call it insane and try to re-establish the old order.

The more violent response comes in the C element of the chiastic structure with the arrival of the scribes from Jerusalem. The response to Jesus' vision and power has become so overwhelming that representatives from the central authority of Judaism make the journey to Galilee to investigate it. If the family thinks he is crazy, the scribes believe that Jesus is evil. Obviously, the religious patterns they see here are not ones they recognize or control. They do not recognize in Jesus' actions the religious world they know. Something is obviously wrong, drastically wrong. They claim that the source of Jesus' power is the devil, through whom Jesus is leading people astray.

Jesus quickly undermines the arguments of the scribes by asking how Satan can survive if he fights against himself. Rather, Satan is that strong man whose house Jesus robs because he has the strength to tie Satan in knots. Jesus not only undercuts the arguments of the scribes but also interprets the nature of his mission so far. He has defeated Satan in the desert (1:12–13) and is now robbing Satan of all the human life that Satan controls and distorts. The battle of the end-time goes on, and Satan is losing badly according to early reports in this section of the gospel.

This story then moves to the mysterious saying of Jesus about the sin against the Holy Spirit, a saying that has been interpreted in many ways to serve many a theological or pastoral interest. If we simply look at the context in which it occurs in this gospel, the meaning is quite clear and direct. People sin against the Holy Spirit when they claim that Jesus is an agent of the kingdom of Satan and that the power behind his mission is evil. The kingdom of God cannot touch the heart that has given up hope and can no longer imagine that God can offer us a different world. One does not sin against the Holy Spirit by committing some particular transgression. Rather a person sins against the Spirit when he thinks that God is too small to be able to deal with our sin and failure. The sin against the Holy Spirit is a failure of the imagination.

The gospel then returns to the B elements of this section. The second part of the account shows Jesus' response to his family. They send a message to him asking to see him. Jesus ignores his physical family, who think he is out of his mind. Jesus respects human freedom. He will not force people to accept his vision and make room for the power of the kingdom of God in their lives. If the human heart is closed, there is nothing Jesus can do to compel a person to follow him. He leaves them to live in their own world.

The last two verses of the chapter, 3:34–35, comprise the second A element of the section. Jesus claims those who do the will of God as his true family. This passage makes the radical quality of discipleship in Mark's gospel apparent. In 1:16–20 the first disciples leave their former way of life and their father to follow Jesus. Now Jesus himself sets the example of leaving one's family behind for the sake of the kingdom. Mark is clearly aware in his own time that the gospel causes social rifts and re-orders human relationships. Even those relationships that hold firm in the light of the gospel, because families and friends accept it together, will be re-founded on a new and deeper basis. Later Peter and the Twelve will raise questions about the great sacrifices they have had to make, but for the present Mark lets us contemplate the tremendous demands of the kingdom.

One element of this section that Roman Catholics find difficult lies in the fact that Mary does not come off particularly well in this gospel. She is a part of the family who do not understand what all this is about and want to bring Jesus under control. Mark may be simply using Mary as a literary figure to emphasize the lack of faith on the part of those who knew Jesus most intimately and yet were blind to what he really was about. Or perhaps Mark was simply unaware of the traditions dealing with Mary that appear in the later gospels. Or finally, perhaps this text reflects tensions in the early Christian community between the very conservative elements of the community led by James, the brother of the Lord, and more liberal elements of the Church who were accepting Gentiles into the church.

Reflections in Front of the Text

In *Foundations of Christian Faith*, the great twentieth-century theologian Karl Rahner speaks of human freedom in terms of creativity rather than choice. In doing so, he runs against the tendency in modern culture to define freedom as choice. We are constantly told that we are free because we can choose to shop at all hours of the night at a local quick mart, because we can fly anywhere we choose in the country whenever we desire, because we can choose this or that soft drink or truck model.

Rahner does not belittle the role of choice in freedom; he just thinks that choice is a secondary and derivative notion of freedom. The deeper sense of human freedom lies in our capacity to transcend what life hands us. The circumstances of our lives and the various events that befall us provide a context in which we construct our lives, but they do not define or determine us. True freedom allows us to take what life hands us, creatively imagine something different, and act to realize those possibilities. The person lying on a deathbed in a hospital room may have far fewer choices than the one who can leave the room to purchase a Pepsi or a Coke and so avoid the reality of death that inhabits the room. But the dying person may have a great deal more freedom by facing impending death in a creative and loving way that involves family and God.

Rahner notes that the most important object of our freedom is not any particular thing in the world that serves as the object of our choices and actions. It is rather our selves as subjects. When we act in the world, we not only shape the world, we shape the persons we are becoming. After twenty years of teaching, a person has become a teacher. It is no longer something he does, it is something he is. A parent becomes a parent by performing day in and day out the many small acts that go into parenting in a loving way. In freedom we not only shape the world of meaning in which we live, we also become persons who reflect the nature of that world of meaning.

In the opening movements of his gospel Mark has placed two worlds before his reader. One is the world we know and are comfortable in; the other is the strange but attractive world of the kingdom of God. Both worlds exercise great power in our lives. The world of the known is comfortable. We know our way around it and it makes a great deal of sense to us. It works. It is the twentieth-century world of North America and Europe, a world of radical individualism, of technology and consumerism, of privatized meaning and values, and of religion that comforts us and affirms the status quo and too rarely bears a prophetic challenge. Living in such a world we become private, technologically savvy consumers.

But the world of the kingdom of God is also inviting. It speaks to the deepest longings and dreams of the human heart. However, the kingdom calls us away from the world of the familiar and from the selves with which we have become comfortable. It calls for conversion of self and world. The gospel summons us to a world of healing and forgiveness. It asks us to leave behind an over-exaggerated sense of the individual and to live in a world in which community and a concern for the common good play a larger part. It shows us that the world is not simply a pile of resources we may consume; it is God's creation and God's gift. We do not own the world; we are a part of God's creation. There is great resistance from our former selves, which must die so that something new can be born in us, and from the former world, which must pass away so that God might call into being a new heaven and new earth.

In the second movement of his gospel Mark asked us to listen to how these two worlds pull at our hearts and minds. Now in the third movement Mark tells us we must choose. Will we become disciples of Jesus and leave the former world behind? Mark gives us the example of two groups who do choose to follow. There are the vast crowds before whom the miracles of the new creation continue to take place. They represent a world that longs for the kingdom of God and is ready to respond to its promises. The second group is that of the Twelve, who serve as paradigms for what the decision to accept the kingdom and follow Jesus means. They serve as a close-up study of the response that is made by the crowds. They represent the cost of discipleship.

The other option held out to us is represented by Jesus' family and the scribes. We can choose to reject Jesus and turn our backs on the promises of the kingdom. Mark quite subtly depicts the reactions of these two groups to Jesus. The world of the kingdom of God is too powerful a reality to be ignored. It must be challenged and explained away because it threatens the status quo. So Mark presents two ways to attack and dismiss it. The opposition claims Jesus and the world in which he lives are either the stuff of madness or are rooted in evil. Both are ways that Jesus' contemporaries used to dismiss him. Both of these strategies are also ways in which the gospel is often dismissed today. We can write it off as crazy, absurd, and impractical. It just doesn't fit with what common sense dictates and with the patterns with which we are comfortable. We can also claim that it is evil. It upsets the established order and does not fit the ways we know that life works.

Both responses are far too common in the church and in secular life. Humanity longs for the kingdom of God and the healing, the justice, the forgiveness, and the peace that only it can bring. Yet both the church and the secular institutions of our world are distrustful of the steps that need to be taken to live in such a way that we are open to and believe in those promises as true possibilities for human life. Toward the end of the cold war those Catholic bishops who opposed the production and deployment of weapons of mass destruction were called hopeless, unpatriotic dreamers. The economic encyclical (*Populorum Progressio*) and pastoral letter (*Octogesimo Adveniens*) on the economy of Paul VI, and the pastoral letter of the American bishops on justice in the economy (*Economic Justice for All*) have had little impact on the world economy. They just don't deal with reality in the minds of the leaders of capitalism.

Karl Rahner would remind us that more than just a choice between two worlds is involved here. The two worlds this section of the gospel puts before us shape us in different ways. What kind of world will we create given the realities that face us? It is a question of imagination. We are always more than the world-as-it-is can encompass. Because we are more than the present world is able to define, the world can always be more than it already is. That is why imagination and the images that guide imagination are so important. They open the possibilities of that something more. Ultimately, in this layer of the gospel Mark puts before his readers the question of which images we will allow to shape our imaginations. For these are the images that will shape what we become and what we will make of the world.

This crucial divide explains why Mark begins the section by mentioning again the many miracles Jesus performed to expunge evil from human hearts and make human lives whole. He hopes we will embrace the kingdom of God.

Key Points for Preaching

This section of the gospel invites homilists to reflect on freedom with their congregations. Mark clearly presents two options and tells his readers stories of those who have made their choice for or against the kingdom of God as it is embodied in the teaching and actions of Jesus. But Mark does more than invite us to choose one path or the other; he pushes our freedom further and asks what we want to become. The Markan summary of 3:7–12 envisions how Jesus can heal us and drive away the evil that plagues us. But the second half of that first A element invites us as disciples to be healers and to cast out evil from the lives of others. It asks us, as disciples, to be agents of change in our world. What do we want to become in our freedom?

This section of the gospel also gives the preacher the opportunity to look at ways the gospel can be dismissed by those whom it threatens. The world of the status quo shapes and shackles our imaginations in powerful ways. Anything that challenges it may look misguided or evil. When Rosa Parks refused to move to the back of a bus in the early days of the civil rights movement in the United States, she was condemned by many Christians not only for breaking the law, but for upsetting the order they thought God had established for society, an order rife with racism. Many admire but few see as wisdom-for-the-world the way of life Mother Teresa and her sisters embrace on the streets of Calcutta. Many see forgiveness as far too risky because of the vulnerability it requires of us. To be a healer you must first recognize that the world is wounded.

This section of the gospel asks the homilist to guide Christian congregations in discernment. What kind of world will we create with the patterns of our lives? What do we see as wisdom and how do we define what is good? What are we becoming through the patterns of our choices?

CHAPTER FOUR

THE MYSTERIOUSNESS OF THE KINGDOM

Mark 4:1–34

There is a history in all men's lives,
Figuring the natures of the times deceas'd;
The which observ'd, a man may prophesy,
With a near aim, of the main chance of things
As yet not come to life, who in their seeds
And weak beginning lie intreasured.
Such things become the hatch and brood of time.

William Shakespeare, second part of *King Henry IV*, III.i.

The World of the Text

Saint Paul told the Romans, "Hope that is seen is not hope" (Rom 8:24, NRSV). But hope has to have some basis. As time passed, the early Christian communities that had made the decision for the gospel began to wonder where the promised kingdom was. Historians think that Mark wrote his gospel either for the Christians in Rome who faced persecutions under the emperor Nero or for communities in northern Galilee and southern Syria who confronted the terrors of the Roman-

Jewish war of 65-70 A.D. In either case, prospects for the kingdom of
God looked rather dim. Perhaps the opponents of the kingdom were
right to consider it madness; perhaps the kingdom had started people
on a path that led to the evil they now faced.

Mark pictures Jesus addressing exactly this issue in the next layer of
his gospel. Those who have contemplated the third box in Mark's puzzle and have opened it by making a decision for Jesus and the kingdom
of God now must wrestle with a new aspect of the mystery of the kingdom. Why does the kingdom seem so small and far away as our daily
lives grind on? Why does the world that stands over against it persist?
What are we to do in the face of such scant evidence for the kingdom?

Mark presents the fourth section of his gospel, 4:1–34, as a sermon
of Jesus that directly addresses these issues. Mark himself composed this
sermon using the traditions about Jesus' teaching that had been handed down to Mark's community. The fact that Jesus is in the boat teaching the crowds, then suddenly talking in private with his disciples, then
back in the boat continuing his sermon to the multitude tells us that
this part of the gospel makes sense to Mark theologically rather than in
the smooth flow of its actions. The sermon bears all the telltale signs of
Mark's style, and it serves well the theological and kerygmatic purposes
of Mark's gospel as a whole. Thus Mark presents not the very words of
Jesus but the impact of his message on an early Christian community.

This sermon should make us sit up and take notice. Time and time
again Mark has told his reader that Jesus taught, but except for the great
proclamation of the kingdom in 1:14–15, we have yet to hear the content of Jesus' teaching. At last Mark is letting us in on the content of
what Jesus had to say about the kingdom. However, by the time we have
read the sermon, we have more questions about the kingdom than
when we began. Jesus' words take us deeper yet into the mystery of the
kingdom, and yet the kingdom remains a mystery.

In piecing together this section of the gospel, Mark uses a variety of
materials, including three parables, an allegorical interpretation of one
of the parables, a collection of pithy sayings of Jesus, and a discussion
about why Jesus uses parables to teach about the kingdom. At first it
appears that Mark has thrown this material together helter-skelter,
whereas in fact he has given it a loose structure which emphasizes the

key points he asks the reader to contemplate in this layer of the gospel. This fourth section of the gospel opens and closes by mentioning several themes. First Mark tells us that Jesus was working with large crowds. Secondly, there is the matter of the boat. As in 3:9, the response to the kingdom has grown so great that the crowds are becoming a problem. In the third chapter Jesus had the disciples ready a boat that they could use to get away if the crowd began to crush Jesus. Now, as the fourth section opens, Jesus must actually use the boat to avoid the crush of such a large number of people. The end of this section of the gospel pictures Jesus and the disciples sailing off in the boat for the other side of the Sea of Galilee. Finally, this layer of the gospel opens and closes with Mark's insisting that Jesus spoke to the masses only in parables. Thus this fourth section of the gospel begins and ends with the mention of the crowds, the fact that the crowds were taught in parables, and the use of the boat. These themes serve as the A elements in a loose chiastic structure that unifies this part of the gospel.

Three seed parables make up the B elements of this section. Mark balances the longer parable of the sower with the shorter parables of the grain growing by itself and of the mustard seed. These three parables constitute the total public teaching of Jesus to the masses.

The C element of the chiastic structure contains the private discussion between Jesus and the disciples about the nature of his teaching and the short mysterious sayings about the lamp and the measuring of wheat. This gives the following loose structure to this section of Mark:

A The boat and the crowds whom Jesus teaches in parables.

    B The parable of the sower.

        C The private discussion of Jesus and his disciples.

    B' Two more seed parables.

A' The boat and the crowds whom Jesus teaches in parables.

The seed parables give us the first clue about the message that this structure is meant to reveal. Most obviously all of the parables mention seeds. We begin with the parable of the sower in 4:3–9, which centers not on the sower but on the seed. The story takes delight in comparing all the obstacles the seed encounters with the amazingly bountiful crop that it finally yields. The sower does not do a particularly good job of getting his crop sown. The birds eat some of it. The scorching sun and weeds take their toll. Some seed finds its way to the roadside where travelers trample it. Yet some seed does land on good soil and produces a harvest of miraculous proportions.

At first glance the farmer in this story does not seem to be doing a very good job. Yet he manages. Through this parable Mark tells his readers that at times God may not seem to be doing a very good job of establishing the kingdom. The seeds of the kingdom are being trampled, scorched, and eaten by those who oppose it. Nero's persecution, the use of Roman legions to quell the Jewish revolt, and the consequent devastation of Palestine all make the kingdom seem like a distant reality. Couldn't God be doing a better job? But the seed finds good soil, and the crop will come. The disciple must learn patient trust in the seeds God has planted.

The parable of the seed in 4:26–29 looks at the same issue from a slightly different perspective. Again the seed does marvelous things, but here the miracle is not the size of the crop but the fact that the seed grows at all. Jesus was a remarkably perceptive man. He must have watched large crops grow from tiny seeds and wondered how this was possible. How does something so great come from something so small? As a first-century man, he did not have a good scientific answer. The growth of large crops from seed is in a way miraculous. But every planting season the human race trusts the miracle and goes out and sows the crops it needs to survive. The human race has learned to trust the seed. Mark wants us to contemplate that trust and then reflect on the seeds of the kingdom. We may not understand how the reality of the kingdom will come about, but we must learn to have faith that in some mysterious way it will.

The parable of the mustard seed in 4:30–32 is another variation on the theme. It contrasts the small size of the original mustard seed with the large shrub it eventually produces. Mark asks us to hold that tiny seed in our hands and contemplate its potential to become the large mustard tree. So too the seeds of the kingdom may seem awfully small at times. We are to hold them in our hands and contemplate the great results they can have in our lives.

At the center of the chiastic structure are the sayings of Jesus that make up his private discussion with the Twelve, the inside group that serves as the model for discipleship. The conversation begins with the Twelve asking him why he speaks in parables to the crowd. Three things follow. First, Jesus tells them that the mystery of the kingdom has been given to them but to others it comes in parables. In the introduction we noted that Mark's use of the singular "mystery" is significant here. In their parallel passages Matthew and Luke use the plural, "mysteries," insisting there are many things to learn about the kingdom. For Mark there is but one thing, one mystery that we must grasp. The whole gospel is written to give us the clues we need to understand that mystery.

Secondly, Jesus says that the kingdom comes in parables to those on the outside. Then he quotes Isaiah 6:9 to say why this is so: that "they may look and see but not perceive, and hear and listen but not understand, in order that they may not be converted and be forgiven" (NAB). This harsh saying leaves both the reader and the preacher wondering what to make of it. In chapter thirteen of his gospel Matthew emphasizes the unforgiving character of the quotation by expanding it to include Isaiah's explanation that the heart of the people has grown fat. This harsh emphasis is absent in Mark's account. In the previous section he has shown us that people are dismissing the message of the kingdom as the stuff of madness or the work the devil. Jesus himself will pay the ultimate penalty for his madness in his execution on the cross. Jews and pagans alike will persecute his followers. The sin against the Holy Spirit is very real in the mind of Mark. Those who have rejected the kingdom as madness or as evil can only hear the gospel as parables, as riddles that make no sense in the world of meaning that dominates the present time.

Thirdly, Jesus offers an allegorical interpretation of the parable in 4:13–20. This interpretation probably reflects the use of the parable in the catechetical work of the early church. Viewed as an allegory, the seeds falling in different places reveal the different responses that greet the Word of God in the lives of Christians. Mark uses this allegorical reading of the parable to emphasize that the kingdom must bear fruit in the life of the disciple. The signs of the arrival and power of the kingdom must become visible in the life of the Christian disciple.

The four short sayings Mark places after the interpretation of the parable contain the heart of the matter in this section of the gospel: the lamp that should not be hidden; things hidden that will finally be made visible; how we are to measure things out; and the mysterious saying that tells us that those who have will be given more. In quick succession these sayings clarify what Mark wants his readers to contemplate. True disciples of Jesus must not hide the lamp of the kingdom. The lamp may seem small now; how it works may seem mysterious to some and crazy to others. But we must trust it and let it shine in our lives. God will not keep it hidden; neither should we. God will ultimately reveal what is hidden and secret now.

How are we to manifest this light? We will make it visible in how we measure things out. The kingdom asks a lot of us. We must leave an old world behind and believe in the vision of a world made evident in the life and the message of Jesus. To have faith is to live as if something else is possible, something different from the world as we now understand it. We measure things out in how we give our lives to this vision of the kingdom. If we are willing to take the risk of living for the sake of the kingdom, the realization of the kingdom in our lives will be great. As we measure out, so shall things be measured back to us in turn. For example, the kingdom promises forgiveness. We measure out our lives by living as if we believed we have been forgiven by God and taking the risk of forgiving others in the same way. Mark believes these tiny acts, these tiny seeds of faith, can change our lives in dramatic ways. Our relationships and our world will become a different place because of the power of the kingdom of God in our lives.

The final saying is puzzling: those who have will be given more, and those who have not will lose what little they already have. Nothing could sound more unchristian. But Mark is not discussing works of charity here or the redistribution of wealth in a search for economic justice. His point is the nature of faith. Faith lives in the light of the promises of the kingdom. It acts as if this strange world of the gospel were true. Faith lived in this way grows as we see the seeds of the kingdom begin to bear fruit. Those without faith, who believe the kingdom is madness, lose what little insight into the kingdom they might have glimpsed in the parables.

Finally, we should note two things about this entire section of the gospel. First, the notion of parable is central. Mark uses the Greek word παραβολη eight times in this section of the gospel. Obviously Mark does not believe we can approach the kingdom directly. Nor can its mystery be simply stated. We must unravel the mystery slowly through the long process of contemplating the various layers of the gospel. Even the Twelve will struggle with the mystery as the gospel narrative progresses. It is difficult to grasp the mystery of the gospel and come to understand the nature of the kingdom. Thus another theme echoes throughout this section: seeing and hearing. Those alert to the kingdom must watch closely to catch the clues. Jesus quotes Isaiah to give the theme its fullest expression: people will look and see but not perceive; they will hear and listen, but not understand. Jesus repeats this theme when he tells the crowds after his first parable: Let those who have ears, hear (4:9). Later he repeats the same admonition to the Twelve after the saying about things hidden and revealed (4:23). Again he repeats the theme in the next sentence, "Take care what you hear" (4:24, NRSV). Hearing and seeing will become major themes of the gospel and shape its central clues.

Reflections in Front of the Text

Often in this life all we have are tiny seeds of what God has promised. The sin and evil in our world provide one reason for this. War and terrorism plague humankind. Racism and sexism diminish us. We tend to take life from others with our jealousies and hatreds, our impatience, and our knack for using people to our own ends. Injustice keeps much of the human race from having the simple necessities of life.

Another reason the kingdom of God can seem so small lies in the fact that life is hard. Sickness robs people of their vitality. Death takes friends and loved ones. Hopes we had cherished as youths fade before the harsh realities of life. We must earn our daily bread by the sweat of our brow.

But the ultimate reason we must deal with seeds is that we are human. To be human is to live in the creative tension between, on the one hand, our infinite potential and longing, and, on the other hand, our limited reality. We possess an infinite capacity to question and seek, to imagine and dream, to love and to hope. But we are also finite and embodied in the here and the now. We desire truth, and ask questions in search of truth that has no limits. But to find truth we must ask particular questions about particular experiences that lead to particular insights. We cannot escape the here and the now, the specific and the contingent. There is no limit to our hunger for beauty, but we only find it before this painting or that sculpture or in listening to that favorite piece of music. Eventually the moment of beauty slips away as other things, necessary things, demand our attention. The human capacity for love knows no limits. But the saddest person is the one who is in love with the idea of love and never gives himself or herself to another individual.

Ultimately we long for God. But we can never possess God as an object among all the other things in our lives. God is present, not as one being among other beings but as Being itself—as the one who makes possible any actual thing. God is like the air we breath—unseen except in its effects; unseen and yet necessary for life. Although unseen, God is present through symbols. Created, limited beings and experiences bear the presence of God, but they are not God. God is present to us and yet beyond us. In this life we get only hints and glimpses of the fullness of God's presence in heaven.

So it is with the kingdom of God. It promises great things. Let us turn again to Hans Küng's description of the kingdom:

> It will be a kingdom where, in accordance with Jesus' prayer, God's name is truly hallowed, his will is done on earth, men (and women) will have everything in abundance, all sin will be forgiven and all evil overcome.
>
> It will be a kingdom where, in accordance with Jesus' promises, the poor, the hungry, those who weep and those who are downtrodden will finally come into their own; where pain, suffering and death will have an end.

These are indeed great hopes, but the realization of these promises can seem so unlikely in actuality. All we see are tiny seeds.

Mark would have us contemplate those seeds. He asks us to hold them dearly in our hearts because they embody what we long for: a moment of peace; an experience of friendship and love; a fair and just solution to some civic or economic conflict; a situation in which the human dignity of all is genuinely respected. Then Mark asks us to take the seed and boldly let it go. We are to cast it out and let it land in new soil. We are to take the risk. The gospel calls us to take our experience of peace and live in a way that allows others to taste it. We must forgive as we are forgiven. We are to act justly and expect justice to grow in the world. We are to take our experiences of the presence of God and share them with others. We do not know whether this seed will find good ground. We cannot fathom how it grows. We cannot understand how something so small will become something large enough to change the world. But we must let go of the seed if the harvest is to have a chance.

Key Points for Preaching

There is a great deal of material here for the homilist. He can invite the congregation to reflect on the seed they hold in their own hearts and hands. Then he can ask them to reflect on why this seed is so precious. The homilist can also ask us to reflect on how others planted those seeds in our lives and how they have grown. The process is often a mystery. But if we reflect on it, we know that the mystery of that growth is real and it works. We have seen wonderful harvests in our own lives.

The real heart of the matter in this section of the gospel, however, lies in the saying, how you measure it out is how it will be measured back. We are not meant to hold seeds in our hands forever. If we keep them in our closed fists long enough, all we eventually have is moldy seed. We must sow the seeds in new soil and trust the mysterious process of God at work in our world. We must trust that there will be a harvest. So the homilist finally must invite the congregation to plant the seeds by living justly, by treating others with dignity, by forgiving, by living peacefully. The harvest will grow, and the kingdom will come if we have faith and live as if its promises are really true.

But all of this comes in parables. Like the early Christians, we opened this section of the gospel with many questions and doubts about the kingdom because its reality seemed so insignificant and distant. After hearing this sermon of Jesus, we are still left with one large mystery. But what is it that makes the kingdom so mysterious? Mark has yet to make that clear to us. For some reason Mark does not think stating the answer directly will work with the crowds. The kingdom harbors a mysterious quality that we can approach only indirectly. We are left wondering what it is about the kingdom that is so difficult to grasp. Perhaps the difficulty lies in the fact that it appears to be so distant and small.

But perhaps the opposite is also true: the promises of God may appear small and distant only because they are not easily perceived and understood. Mark himself may be asking the same question in this chapter when he wonders why the kingdom has not found wider acceptance and so transformed human life more profoundly. The mysterious character of the kingdom makes it hard to believe in it and trust it with our lives. Part of the task of the homilist is to help Christians see how the seeds that are already planted in our lives have the power to grow.

Mark's gospel does more than just challenge us to live according to our understanding of the kingdom. It summons us to struggle to perceive and understand what the kingdom means. To be a disciple is to be one who is caught up in this one great mystery. Therefore Mark begs his readers to pay close attention to the clues. Mark repeats the command to listen in 4:3, 9, 23, and 24. He tells us in 4:12 that the difficulty in understanding the kingdom has to do with the ability to listen, and so in the fourth section he keeps repeating the command to listen. As the gospel develops we must watch to see who can see and hear.

One clue to the mystery lies in how Jesus teaches. So far Jesus has taught at many points in Mark's gospel, but we were never told the content of that teaching. The actions of Jesus that surround the statements about his teaching carry the lessons of the gospel. Perhaps it is only through our own actions that we will come to know the secret of the kingdom. Action may be the key, the only way to learn. The kingdom cannot be communicated in words. But what is it that is so hard to hear and learn? The heart of this section of the gospel lies in the statement about how we measure things out. We will find what we hope for only in giving it to others. That is what is hard to hear and understand.

Part of the challenge of preaching the fourth section of Mark's gospel is to renew the promises of the first chapter. The fourth layer of the gospel emphasizes again the promises of the kingdom and calls readers to trust them and build their lives on them. But this reiteration of the gospel takes place in a new setting that takes us deeper into the mystery of the kingdom. The initial excitement and the triumphant re-creative march of God through human life in chapter one have given way to a more sober analysis of the kingdom in the present world. The kingdom faces opposition and seems to be a pale, distant reality. Early enthusiasm for it must mature into a faith that remains rooted in the kingdom in spite of opposition and its seeming insignificance in the affairs of our world.

How we act now on the basis of our having heard the promises will determine how we experience the kingdom later when it is fully manifest. Those who give generously to the kingdom by living in the light of its promises will experience the realization of the kingdom in its fullness. Those who hold back and hedge their bets because the kingdom seems to be such a long shot will have what little of it they have experienced taken away. The only way to share in the reality of the kingdom is to live now as if it were a real possibility.

The seed parables contain three important lessons for a community which is beginning to have doubts and questions about the kingdom in the face of suffering and opposition. First, like the harvest of the seed, the kingdom will come in its inevitable and miraculous way. Ultimately the promises are in God's hands, not ours, and God's promises will not fail. Secondly, even though the reality of the kingdom may seem small and insignificant in the present, its eventual reality will be miraculously great. Other issues, other forces, other spheres of life may seem to dwarf the kingdom as we know it now, but we must trust it and live as if it were the one and only reality that makes any true difference in life. Thirdly, though the kingdom may be facing great opposition in the present, it will prevail. The forces in life that distract from it, that oppose its vision, and that call us as disciples to put our faith in something other than the kingdom will give way eventually to the miraculous harvest. As seeds give way to wheat, so promises of the kingdom become reality.

CHAPTER FIVE

THE POWER OF THE KINGDOM

Mark 4:35–5:43

Ah, the thunder of many peoples
They thunder like the thundering of the sea!
Ah, the roar of the nations,
They roar like the roaring of mighty waters!
The nations roar like the roaring of many waters,
But he will rebuke them, and they will flee away.

Isaiah 17:12–13 (NRSV)

Then the Lord addressed Job out of the storm and said:
Who is this that obscures divine plans with words of ignorance?
Gird up your loins now, like a man;
I will question you, and you tell me the answers!
Who shut the sea in with doors when it burst out of the womb?—
When I made the clouds its garment
And thick darkness its swaddling band,
And prescribed bounds for it
And set bars and doors and said

"Thus far shall you come, and no farther,
and here shall your proud waves be stopped"?

Job 38:1-3, 8-11 (NAB and NRSV)

The World of the Text

Words make sentences but actions speak volumes. If the sermon in the fourth section of the gospel addressed the concerns of Jesus' followers about how small the kingdom appears to be and yet how great it will become, the actions of Jesus in the fifth section of the gospel magnify the themes of the sermon on a grand scale. Having broken open the box that held the parables in the last section, Mark now presents his reader with four of the most dramatic miracles in the gospel. These miracles present in action the themes the parables had only spoken of in the last section. The situations Jesus addresses are desperate, and the possibilities of the kingdom must seem distant and small indeed to those involved in them. But they trust. They plant the seeds of hope in how they deal with their situations, and they see the kingdom come to fruition in their lives. Section five of the gospel thus echoes the theme of the power of the kingdom to change human life.

The first miracle, the calming of the storm in 4:35-41, has several moments laden with meaning. First there is the symbolism of the storm. This is not just a nature miracle in which Jesus shows his power over the forces of the natural world. Mark makes much greater claims for Jesus and the kingdom. Mark's frame of reference goes all the way back to the first chapter of Genesis where God brought the order of creation out of primeval chaos. In ancient Hebrew thinking God did not create out of nothing. The concept of nothing had not even been developed by the pragmatic mind of the ancient Hebrews but had to await the influence of Hellenistic philosophy to find its way into Jewish and Christian traditions. The ancient Hebrews thought of creation as the act that brought order out of chaos. Watery storms served as the great symbol for chaos. Thus as God begins to create in Genesis 1, God's Spirit hovers over the formless void of the waters. Likewise, when Jesus finally awakens to face the storm, he repeats the action of God at the dawn of creation; he faces the forces of chaos that stand in the way of God's creative activity. The kingdom that appeared to be so weak bears the very power of the creator God who calls all things into being and rules the entire universe. The disciples ask the right question: "Who can this be? Even the wind and the sea obey him."

A second meaning of the miracle lies in the fact that Mark sees it as an exorcism. When Mark reports that Jesus rebuked the winds, he uses the same Greek word (επιτιμαω, to rebuke) that he used to describe Jesus' rebuke of the demons in 1:25 and 3:12. His command to silence the storm also echoes the command that silences the demon in 1:25. This miracle reveals that the kingdom commands a power great enough to conquer the evil that storms through human history. Mark invites his reader to reflect on the strength of chaos and evil in human life in war, in destructive human relationships, in systemic injustice, in the false values that can lead a people astray from their humanity. He then points out that the kingdom in Jesus can conquer any chaos and any evil. It bears the very power of the creator.

A third feature of this story takes us back to section four of the gospel and the issue of how hard it is to apprehend to the kingdom. The characters in the gospel as well as those who read Mark's account find the kingdom difficult to grasp. It comes in parables that seem like riddles. But Jesus does not use parables to reveal the kingdom to the Twelve. He discusses it openly and directly with them. By watching the disciples handle this mystery we should be able to come to a deeper understanding ourselves. However, the disciples are not doing well at all. In 4:13 Jesus asked them whether or not they were capable of understanding any of the parables. Here in their first test after Jesus' sermon, they utterly fail to grasp what is going on. Jesus' question in 4:40 is even more serious than the one asked in 4:13, for he asks them if they have no faith at all. If these insiders, who are getting special help from Jesus, struggle with the mystery of the kingdom, how hard it must be for us to apprehend the kingdom and build our lives on its promises. What is it that continues to be a stumbling block not only for them, but also for us?

The last thing to note about this story is that it takes place in the boat as Jesus and the disciples are crossing the Sea of Galilee. This body of water separated Jewish Galilee from the gentile territory of the Decapolis. In this section Mark begins to use the boat for theological purposes. The boat will now be taking Jesus back and forth between Jewish and gentile territory and bridging the gap between these two peoples. The kingdom is about to spread into new territory, that of the Gentiles whom the Jews had not expected to be admitted to the kingdom of God. In the second section (4:38–40) the gospel concentrated on the tensions that arose over the issues of whether the kingdom could include sinners and what kind of a God it is that would want to include them. Those tensions now heighten as Jesus includes not only sinners but Gentiles as well. It is significant that the disciples fail to comprehend the kingdom while they are in the boat on the way to gentile territory. Perhaps this inclusive nature of the kingdom proved to be a stumbling block not only to the Jews of Jesus' time but also to Mark's community. Might it not challenge us as well?

The second miracle, the healing of the Gerasene demoniac, belongs with the calming of the storm at sea. One interprets the other. Both the themes of overcoming chaos and the inclusion of the Gentiles lie at the heart of the exorcism of the Gerasene demoniac in 5:1–20. We are clearly in gentile territory, not only geographically by the crossing of the lake, but culturally and religiously with the emphasis on the herd of pigs. A good Jew would have nothing to do with pork, either on the hoof or on his plate. Jesus, however, does not hesitate to enter a situation that would make him religiously unclean and unacceptable if he must do so to help this possessed man.

Again we find Jesus facing chaos as he did with the storm at sea. This time the chaotic elements rage within the human heart and mind of this possessed man. They rage with such power that the distraught man has been driven into the abode of the dead. He lives among the tombs outside the town. Some uncontrollable, chaotic element in this man's life has overwhelmed his spirit. The ordered human world cannot contain him. In many ways this chaos in the realm of the human spirit is far more frightening and destructive than that which the elements of nature can produce. Jesus, however, remains in control and is able to restore the man to wholeness. The fact that the demons of chaos enter the pigs and the pigs destroy themselves in the lake only serves to emphasize the chaos of the kingdom of Satan that Jesus conquers in this situation.

The healing of the Gerasene demoniac is the first miracle Jesus performs in Gentile territory. It parallels the first miracle he performed in Jewish territory, in which Jesus cast out a demon from a possessed man in the synagogue in Capernaum. Mark will continue this kind of parallelism in order to emphasize the inclusion of the Gentiles in the kingdom of God.

A further parallelism follows this first Gentile miracle. Just as Jesus had performed the first miracle of the gospel for the sake of a man and followed it with the healing of a woman, so too Jesus follows this first gentile miracle with powerful deeds carried out for the sake of two women. Mark's concern about the inclusion of the Gentiles complements his concern about the inclusion of women. In dealing with women Jesus is breaking down religious and cultural barriers that had kept women religiously and culturally subordinate. He demonstrates concretely that God does not discriminate among his people on the basis of gender.

Mark organizes the stories of these two women in 5:21–43 in a chiastic structure which runs A B A'. The two A elements comprise the story of the raising of the daughter of Jairus, the synagogue official. The B element, which is the story of the healing of the woman with the hemorrhage, interrupts the two parts of the A story. Thus Mark uses the two stories to reinforce and interpret each other.

The story of the woman with the hemorrhage contains many of the elements of the story of the cure of the leper in chapter one. The woman has some sort of trouble with menstrual flow so that her constant bleeding not only causes her physical problems but also makes her religiously unclean and therefore communally unacceptable. Anything or anyone she touches becomes unclean. In healing her Jesus not only cures her physical ailment but also shows that she is religiously and socially acceptable. Mark brings out the drama of the situation by letting the reader see the struggle the woman undergoes in order to reach out and touch Jesus. She has to have enough faith in the promises of the kingdom to break the religious and social taboos that did not allow a woman, and a religiously unclean person at that, to reach out and touch a man. She is frightened and trembling, which in Mark is a typical response to the risk that the kingdom asks people to make. But in spite of her fear, she acts on the basis of the promises and is touched by the healing power of the kingdom.

The story of the raising of Jairus' daughter encloses the story of the unclean, bleeding woman. Again the issue of ritual impurity dominates the story, for contact with the corpse of the little girl would make Jesus unclean. Like the story it surrounds, this passage illustrates faith overcoming fear as people learn to entrust their lives to the promises God has made. This story takes the power of faith to new level, however, for it shows that Jesus can conquer death itself. The Greek for the action of the little girl in 5:42, ανεστη (to rise up), is the verb that Mark uses to speak of the resurrection in the predictions of the death and resurrection of Jesus later in the gospel. In this miracle Mark gives us early hints that even death itself cannot stand in the way of the kingdom.

The story of the raising of Jairus' daughter also reflects the negative responses the gospel has evoked. When Jesus tells the mourners gathered in the home that the girl is asleep, not dead, they laugh at him. Once again, to outsiders the seeds of the kingdom seem like sheer madness.

Reflections in Front of the Text

Worlds of meaning need maintenance. In his book *Myth and Reality*, Mircea Eliade relates how peoples who live in mythic cultures maintain their symbolic worlds on a large scale through rituals of renewal in their yearly cycles of feasts and on a small scale in the rituals that fill their everyday lives. In *The Social Construction of Reality*, Peter Berger and Thomas Luckman describe similar processes for religious and secular societies. They hold that all societies have a need to maintain their worlds of meaning both subjectively and objectively. Objectively they do so by institutionalizing such social functions as government, education, health care, and science. Subjectively they sustain their worlds through everyday routines and conversations. In this way they are able, without any need for reflection, to negotiate their way through a complicated pattern of social organization and the understanding of the world that provides the basis for that organization.

Modern secular societies may believe that they have banished myths from their worlds, but they stand just as much in need of world-renewing rituals as any ancient tribe. The people of the United States of America renew their fundamental sense of themselves and their social world every Fourth of July and Inauguration day. Every spring in the Easter Vigil Christians renew their world by participating in the founding events of the Paschal mystery.

If people do not maintain the symbolic world of meaning in which they live, chaos can threaten it. Chaos also threatens when worlds of meaning collide. That is the theme Mark asked us to contemplate in the second layer of his gospel, which told us that we could not put new wine into old wineskins. Here in the fifth section about the mystery of the kingdom, Mark returns to that theme of the threatening chaos, but he encourages further reflection by asking us to contemplate how we can face that chaos when the seeds of the new world we hope to embrace seem so small and ineffectual in the face of powerful opposing forces. In this section Mark presents us with some of the most dramatic miracles in his gospel, stories which contain at their core a struggle with chaos.

The central element in the chiastic structure of this section of the gospel, the story of the woman with the hemorrhage, provides the primary focus of this struggle. One small gesture, her touching Jesus' cloak, provides the key to the woman's story. It is a ritual gesture that counters and challenges rather than maintains the world in which she finds herself. By stepping outside the bounds of her people's symbolic world, this simple act sets worlds reeling in a storm that shakes the very foundations of the cosmos as she and her people understood it. By touching Jesus' cloak the woman calls into question that world's essential distinction between the clean and the unclean. The world of first-century Judaism considered her unclean because of her irregular menstrual bleeding. Anything she touched became tainted by her uncleanness. Her predicament recalls that of the leper of the first chapter. Both are already dead socially. They dare not mix in society in normal ways for fear they will bring disease and dreaded uncleanness into people's lives. Her gesture challenges that way of looking at herself. It defies the religion and the society that sees her and the world in terms of what is clean and unclean. It questions a view of God who would find her unacceptable because of her physical condition.

I doubt this woman could have fully appreciated all that the kingdom of God means. She just knew that the world in which she lived no longer made sense. She heard Jesus speak of a new world in which she could be healed, in which God loved her just as she was, and in which the distinction of what was ritually clean and unclean was no longer significant. She heard this promise and she planted a seed by acting as if something different were possible for her because of the presence of Jesus and the power of the kingdom. She touched Jesus' cloak, a gesture that made sense only in that new world of the kingdom, and she enters that kingdom. God re-created the human landscape of her life.

Other people are planting seeds in these stories. Jairus, the synagogue official, also takes a serious risk. In chapter two Mark told us that scribes were questioning the ministry of Jesus, saying that his presumption that he could forgive sins was blasphemy (2:7). By chapter three the Pharisees view Jesus as a great enough threat that they were conspiring with the Herodians to find a way to destroy him (3:6). Later in the third chapter the scribes were telling people that Jesus was evil and his power came from Satan (3:22). This father risks public action that flies in the face of this assessment of Jesus by the leaders of his religion. He asks Jesus to heal his dying daughter. Like the woman with the hemorrhage, he faces a desperate situation and dares to disrupt the tidy world of officialdom.

The woman was an outcast because of her physical condition. Jairus is about to lose someone he loves deeply. So he plants a seed and takes a gamble on the new world of the kingdom that Jesus proclaimed. Jairus' faith looks ridiculous to those gathered in his home to support him. His daughter has died, and in the perspective of an old world nothing more can be done. Death has the final word. Jesus says no, something else is possible, for she only sleeps. The people laugh at this assessment of the situation and what they think is possible in it. The synagogue official plants a seed that produces a great harvest. For the power of the kingdom working in Jesus restores his daughter to life. Death does not have the final word in the kingdom of God. Resurrection is possible for those who put their faith in Jesus and live as if his promises are believable.

These two small gestures, touching the cloak of Jesus and daring to ask Jesus to heal the little girl, both embrace the possibility of a new and different world. They represent the gestures which planted seeds in the lives of all those whom the power of the kingdom touched through the ministry of Jesus. All those whom Jesus healed, all those from whom he cast out the power of Satan, had to have planted seeds in similar ways with small gestures of hope that a different world was possible than the one in which they were imprisoned.

But these gestures unleashed the storms of chaos. These storms were both objective and subjective. The challenge to the given order disturbed the objective world of society so that the very foundations of nature seemed to be shaken to their core in the storm at sea. The storms also raged in people's hearts and minds, as we saw in the story of the Gerasene demoniac. All of these events must have raised disturbing questions for people. They must have caused confusion and disorientation. No wonder the authorities felt they must speak out against what they saw as an evil disruption of the order God had in mind when God created the world. They had to act to put an end to Jesus and his work. But the reaction of the Jewish authorities only added to the questions and confusion people were facing.

Small seeds were producing great storms. They were challenging worlds that many thought were set firmly on their foundations. Small seeds can do that. Simple gestures can change a life or a world. President Nixon changed years of American foreign policy by the simple gesture of making an official trip to Red China. In doing so he asked Americans to think differently about the world and our relationships to a people we viewed as the enemy. Rosa Parks refused to obey the law and move to the back of a bus in racially charged Alabama. Her gesture challenged the world as she knew it and asked if something else were not possible. How should we view ourselves and those whose skins are different from our own? What does a just society look like? Rosa Parks' questions unleashed social storms that are still with us.

Those who forgive plant a small seed. They take the risk of looking at themselves and the ones who hurt them in a different light. They illumine the shadows of resentment and revenge that haunt our world. Those who trust the abundance of what God has given them in creation and share with those in need risk a bit of their own wealth and trust that a different world is possible. Those who seek to live a bit more simply and turn their backs on the culture of consumerism risk not fitting in a world where possessions define people. All are small steps. All can cause storms in individual lives and in society, for they risk the chaos of leaving an old familiar world behind and embracing a new world only dimly perceived.

Meanwhile Jesus is asleep in the back of the boat. He is the cause and center of the storm, but he is at peace. When the disciples, who are beginning to fear for their lives in the midst of the chaos (5:38–40), awaken him, Jesus questions whether they have faith. This inner group of disciples deserves the reader's close attention for through them Mark gives us a detailed picture of the dynamics of hearing the proclamation of the kingdom and responding in faith. In this section fear swamps the disciples. The chaos seems powerful enough to overwhelm them totally. Mark has not yet made it completely clear why this is so. A part of the reason is objective. The strong opposition of the scribes and the Pharisees, who hold authority in their world, inspires fear. A part of the reason is subjective. The disciples must have had their own questions and doubts about the whole enterprise when all they hold in their hands are the seeds of the promise of a new world.

Some of the opposition and some of their own doubts must have had roots in the theological meaning of the boat they found themselves in. That boat brought Jews and Gentiles together in response to the ministry of Jesus. Jesus' sharing of the reality of the kingdom with the Gentiles must have shaken their view of God and of the boundaries of the Jewish social world in which they felt comfortable. Disturbed and shaken, they have every right to question and doubt and even to fear where all this might lead. But they stay with Jesus. They provide a good model for any disciple of Jesus.

Fears and questions do not disqualify one from discipleship. But if fear keeps us out of the boat so that we can protect a prejudice against those who are different, we will find the seed of our faith to be the kind that sprouts quickly and withers in the face of consequences we had not foreseen. Questions and doubts are a part of the journey any disciple must embark on. Embracing the kingdom may not be the madness that some critics of the kingdom think, but it might be madness not to quake a bit at the change the kingdom demands. Fear need not disqualify one from discipleship. In fact one might well be disqualified by not having fear in the face of the change that causes chaos.

Key Points for Preaching

The central focus of this section of the gospel is the contrast between the desperate situations people often face and the power of the kingdom of God to bring wholeness to human life. In treating the stories of this section of the gospel, homilists have the task of contemplating with the congregation those extremes in our own lives. The stories of the gospel find parallels in our own lives when we face serious illness and the death of loved ones. They are present in the prejudices that distort our society and the hatred that separates peoples. They are present in the blindness or hypocrisy of institutions that do not serve the needs of society but seek their own ends. Leaders of church communities do not have to look far to find situations like those Jesus faced in this section of the gospel.

The key gesture of this section of the gospel belongs to the woman with the hemorrhage who reaches out and touches Jesus in spite of the fact that her entire world of meaning tells her that what she is doing is wrong. We can open a new world of possibilities with simple acts. All we need is a small seed of faith. That seed might be a quiet affirmation of life in a cancer patient's room, a simple act of kindness that recognizes the dignity and equality of another person, or an act of reconciliation toward an estranged friend. Such gestures have the power to open new possibilities of life. Homilists have the chance in this section of the gospel to face hard situations with their congregations and contemplate what gestures might open new worlds.

The homilist can also deal with the chaos that lies between worlds. A fundamental change of perspective must occur if we are to let go of despair and embrace life. The way we look at the world can often harbor prejudices, injuries, and hatreds. Letting go of that old world is risky, because up till now we have known only that old world. As disciples of Jesus, we may find ourselves at sea facing strong storms in our hearts. In those moments we need to hear stories of how powerful the Word of God can be in calming the storms and reordering the world.

CHAPTER SIX

FURTHER REFLECTIONS ON DISCIPLESHIP

Mark 6:1–30

I have often thought upon death,
And I find it the least of all evils.

Francis Bacon, *An Essay on Death*

The World of the Text

Confusion and doubt are a part of life and a part of discipleship. Mark makes that clear in the last section of the gospel. Now in the sixth section of the gospel he looks at some old issues in new ways. We have broken open the box that held the great miracles of chapters four and five, and we hold in our hands yet another box, the sixth, which looks curiously like the third. Its clues to the mystery of the kingdom recall those of the third section of the gospel. It contrasts the response to the kingdom on the part of two groups, and it asks again the question, who will follow? Like the third section, this new layer of the gospel follows a section in which anyone who would follow Jesus is caught in the chaos between two worlds. But Mark not only asks us to contemplate these questions again; he also adds some important nuances.

This next section is short and its organization is simple. Mark compares two familiar groups: Jesus' family, which in this section he expands to include the hometown folk, and those who follow Jesus, which he represents by the Twelve. Mark contrasts them by telling a story about the response of each. However, Mark introduces fresh nuances to the theme of discipleship by casting the story of the response of the disciples in a chiastic structure. The A elements tell the story of the sending out of the disciples on a missionary journey and their return. The B element comments on this with the story of the beheading of John the Baptist. Clearly there are new elements of discipleship for the reader to contemplate.

As the section opens, Jesus has returned home with his disciples. On the Sabbath he was teaching in the synagogue with such wisdom that he amazed his family and neighbors.

Typical of Mark, the story does not tell us the content of that synagogue session. As readers, we must understand the teaching of Jesus in the context of his actions. Here the teaching of Jesus reflects the great miracles of the last section and the decision his followers must make to trust the kingdom of God. In the story of the first missionary journey of the disciples, Mark wants us to keep in mind the stories of the power of the kingdom in the face of desperate situations.

At first the hometown folk stand in awe of all that Jesus has done and taught. Who would not be amazed at the power of the kingdom displayed in the work of Jesus? But then the questions and doubts in the face of chaos take over. People who have known Jesus from boyhood respond to his teaching by asking where this local man got all this authority. They know him, after all. If tradition is correct, for thirty years or so they had watched him grow up and work in their midst. They know his roots. Where would a carpenter's son come up with these ideas and this kind of power? It is all too much for them, and they write off Jesus by reducing him to what they have known, a local craftsman and nothing more. They will not accept him.

Jesus in his turn is amazed at them. Mark uses a small chiastic structure here that brackets the response of the hometown people with their amazement at the beginning and Jesus' amazement at the end. Jesus quotes the proverb that a prophet is not welcomed in his home town and among his family. Mark notes that Jesus could work no miracles there except a few healings. The problem was their lack of faith.

The major structural element of this section of the gospel is the comparison of the disciples' reaction to the negative response of the people of Nazareth. In the last section we saw that the disciples are not immune to the same kinds of questions, doubts, and fears that others face. They differ, however, because they take the risk of embracing the new world of the kingdom. They plant the seed by accepting the promises of the kingdom. This section takes us further into their response and adds a new dimension to discipleship. The follower of Jesus responds in faith not only by living as if the promises of the kingdom are for real but also by proclaiming the kingdom to others as Jesus did. Faith is not a private matter meant to change the life of the individual only. It calls us to proclaim the gospel so that it might change the world. This is clear in Mark's story of the first missionary journey of the Twelve.

What is remarkable about this journey is the charge that Jesus gives to the Twelve. They are to do everything he has done. Jesus' ministry up to this point has been one of preaching the kingdom, healing, and casting out demons. The disciples are to do the same. Jesus gives them power over unclean spirits, and so they share the power that Jesus won in the desert with his victory over Satan. They anoint people and cure them. And they preach repentance, which we have seen is a reorientation of a person's life in the light of the proclamation of the kingdom.

The disciples share in the ministry of Jesus with a minimum of equipment. They are to travel light. They take no bread, no backpack, no money, no spare clothing. They are to rely on those who welcome the message of the kingdom.

Urgency pervades these instructions, an urgency that echoes throughout the gospel. The Greek in which the gospel was written carries this urgency in its breathless telling of one story after another, connecting them with the words "and then...and then...and then...." Unlike Matthew and Luke, Mark thinks there is little time left to accomplish the preaching of the kingdom. The time is at hand and now is the hour. Disciples must be single-minded given the lateness of the hour. There is a radical quality, too, about the call of the gospel in Mark. If you giv' yourself to the gospel, you do not have much room for other concer'

In the story of the missionary journey of the disciples, Mark pictures their work as paralleling and imitating in all of its details the work of Jesus. Between the departure of the Twelve and their return, Mark tells the story of another person whose life parallels that of Jesus, John the Baptist. Like Jesus, he preached. His was a message of expectation, while that of Jesus was one of fulfillment. Like Jesus, John seems to have gotten into trouble with the authorities, in John's case with Herod Antipas. Both were handed over. The Greek is very clear. It uses the same word, παραδιδωμι (to hand over), in three places: in 1:14, where it says that John had been arrested; in 9:31, in the second passion prediction in which Jesus says he will be handed over; and in 13:9, where Jesus gives the disciples the disturbing news that they too will be handed over. This parallelism in the use of the Greek word παραδιδωμι is mirrored in the chiastic structure in which the story of the missionary journey of the Twelve surrounds the story of the death of John the Baptist. The disciples risk losing their lives just like Jesus and John the Baptist before them. They too will be handed over.

Here we finally get a clear picture of the greatest stumbling block to accepting the reality of the kingdom. It involves persecution and possibly death. Is it any wonder the disciples were fearful of the chaos that rocked the boat in chapter five? Mark has hinted at this fear a number of times. He relates that John was handed over in 1:14 and that the Pharisees and Herodians were plotting against Jesus in 3:6. He tells us about the negative campaign the opponents of Jesus were mounting against his teaching and work, in which they claimed Jesus' message was evil and madness. Now the issue is out in the open: to embrace the kingdom could involve losing your life.

In this section Mark also begins to prepare his readers for the death of Jesus. What happened to John will happen to Jesus. But that is not the end of the kingdom. Jesus begins to hand his work over to the disciples. They are the ones who must carry it on after his death and resurrection. ᵗ ᵗch of the four canonical gospels had to deal with the simple but ᵗ questions that faced the early Christian community: where is ᵗnd how does his work continue? Matthew begins and ends ᵗ the proclamation that Jesus is God with us; he is with ᵗe world. In the story of the disciples on the road to

Emmaus, Luke emphasizes that where the Church does the work of Jesus and welcomes the stranger as Jesus did, our eyes are opened and we recognize him in our midst. For John a mystical relationship exists between the risen Jesus and the disciples so that Jesus abides in them. Mark places the emphasis on the second coming of Jesus. Mark's is a radically eschatological gospel in which time is short and the Lord will return soon. But the work of the kingdom must go on. Therefore he pictures Jesus beginning to prepare his disciples for the reality of his death and resurrection by handing over to them the work of the kingdom. God's promise must work in them as it does in Jesus.

Reflections in Front of the Text

This rather short section of the gospel offers a great deal of material for reflection and preaching.

We have seen in our reflections on section three that Karl Rahner defines freedom not so much in terms of what we choose to do, but in what we make of ourselves through our choices and actions. He goes further than this and speaks of the self we create as something eternal.

Freedom is the event of something eternal. But since we ourselves are still coming to be in freedom, we do not exist with and behold this eternity, but in our passage through the multiplicity of the temporal we are performing this event of freedom, we are forming the eternity which we ourselves are and are becoming. (*Foundations*, p. 96)

Since in this life we do not exist with and behold this eternity, only in death does the work of our freedom find completion. In death we offer our lives in their finality to God. You could argue that the ultimate act of freedom for an individual is the act of dying, in which we bring our lives to completion and give ourselves to God. Rahner says as much in an earlier essay:

Through death—and not after it—*there is* (not: begins to be) the achieved definitiveness of the freely matured existence of man. What has come to be is there as the hard won and untrammeled validity of what was once temporal; it has progressed as spirit and freedom, in order to be. ("The Life of the Dead," *Theological Investigations*, vol. IV)

This section of Mark takes us back to the central theme of the thir section, the choice of whether to embrace the kingdom Jesus proclaims or to write it off as madness or evil. But in this box of the puzzle, which lies at a deeper level and thus closer to the heart of the mystery, death raises its head. Death becomes a real possibility if we choose the kingdom. It happened to John. Mark's story inevitably leads to the death of Jesus. How can the disciple hope to avoid it?

But as Rahner points out, death is the culmination and validation of a life for all eternity. The question then becomes, what do we want to be eternally and how do we fashion that eternal reality by how we live in this world now? No one is condemned to hell. We create it and choose it for ourselves. The proclamation of the kingdom not only opens a new world to us in the present, in time. It opens different kinds of eternity we can create and choose. The choices lie before us: bitterness over past injuries or forgiveness; a world filled with hatred and war or a world shaped by a peace founded on justice; living in the alienation which our prejudices produce or embracing others who are different as a part of our common human community. The people of Jesus' home town made the choice of writing off the kingdom as folly and evil. In the face of the question of which world we want to shape for ourselves for eternity, we might now ask which choice looks like madness or evil to us.

Given the specter of death that appears in this section, we must read the section in the light of the one that precedes it. In section five we examined the story of Jesus' raising the synagogue leader's daughter from death. Death does not win the final victory, life does. Jesus did not conquer Satan and evil merely in the desert. He defeats all that robs humanity of life at any time. Confidence in this victory gives the disciple the courage to face the doubts, the fears, and the opposition the kingdom raises.

Mark adds another dimension to the choice for discipleship in this layer by proclaiming that the choice we make is not simply for ourselves. We do not take the leap of faith that the promises of the king-
are for real for ourselves only. We do so for the sake of others as
ich is why Mark insists in this section that discipleship involves
disciple of Jesus proclaims the kingdom of God. In Mark's
unity which thought the end of time was near, that deci-
ood many of the baptized would have been involved

in the missionary work of the church because the gospel had a certain urgency to it. We now know we have more time than the early Church originally thought. But we must not lose sight of the connection between baptism, discipleship, and mission.

Not all of the baptized will undertake missionary journeys or take up preaching formally. But our lives should proclaim the kingdom of God. The way that we live ought to make visible the promises of the kingdom by showing others the seeds of what is possible. The actions that proclaim the kingdom need not be great. The woman with the hemorrhage in chapter five merely reached out and touched Jesus' cloak. But that was a gesture that changed her life and shook worlds to their foundations. A life of faithfulness to the promises of the kingdom speaks loudly in a world that sees such gestures as evil and mad.

Mark also asks us to reflect on the nature of miracles in this section. We usually think of miracles as acts of God which set aside the natural order of things so that God may accomplish something that is not possible in that natural order. The ancient world, however, did not view miracles in the same way. The ancients did not distinguish between the natural and the supernatural order of things as we do. Heaven and earth were of a piece, and something as simple as a seed becoming a great plant could manifest the power of God. Some things were clearly out of the ordinary, and they were quickly attributed to God or to Satan. But God was not as removed from daily life as some today think.

Miracles, then, were not simply a powerful contradiction of nature. They were marvelous acts of God which brought about life in ways that were beyond what we think possible. But in the gospels God does not step in arbitrarily. God respects the freedom of people. Some kind of trust, some faith must open the life of a person to the power of God to move in new ways. The initiative does not lie with the human. God offers a new life; God promises what is possible in the kingdom. God even acts in mysterious ways we do not perceive or understand in order to move the human heart. But human persons ultimately must entrust their lives to God. Freedom is a precious gift God has given us. God respects it and lets divine power be limited by human freedom. Therefore, where there is no faith, Jesus is not able to work a miracle The faith that is missing is a trust in those promises, a trust that le?

an individual to live as if the promises can become a reality.

In this section Mark raises three issues that might keep a person from faith. One is familiarity. The people of Jesus' home town are able to dismiss Jesus and his proclamation of the kingdom because they just know him too well. The dynamics of this are fascinating. The message of Jesus bears an extraordinary invitation to a new world of possibility for human life. His actions, especially in the previous section, realize those promises in extraordinary ways for people who face hopeless situations. And yet Jesus' neighbors write it off with a simple, "Oh, he's just the carpenter's son." The gospel makes some very astonishing claims. The world that it opens to us is the stuff of dreams. The challenges the gospel makes are daunting; they shake the characters in Mark's gospel to their roots. Yet the gospel can often become too familiar. We have heard it too often and assume we know its message. We have tamed it and go about our daily lives without letting its promise touch on us or its vision disturb us. If we find that the gospel is no longer disturbing, it has ceased to be gospel.

Our possessions place another obstacle in the path to faith. Jesus sent his first missionaries out without money, food, or extra clothing. In Mark's understanding of history, time is running out. Urgency pervades his gospel. We see things today from a different temporal perspective. And so we have had to take things like food, clothing, shelter, and money seriously. But we can also get too comfortable in the world as we now know it. The things we own and our worries about them can slip into the center of our hearts. We can become obsessed with things. The vision of what the world would be like without them could disturb many. What we own and what we desire to own keep us from embracing the gospel that promises us a richer life based on realities that bring true happiness and that do not die. The familiar life in which we now find ourselves comfortable may keep us from life in its fullness.

Thirdly, Mark asks us to contemplate the inclusion of the Gentiles as ʼʼstacle to the gospel. Mark places the final schism between Jesus ʼʼmily right after Jesus has broken through the barrier that sep- ʼʼvs and the Gentiles. This inclusivity was too much for some ʼʼw Jesus, and it could well be the teaching that the peo- ʼʼown found so amazing. We do know that the issue of how to include the Gentiles shook the early church to its core. In the next section Mark will speak to the issue in such a way that it leads the reader to suspect that his own community struggled with the question. Mark is clear in what he thinks about the matter. The kingdom comes before everything, and it banishes all distinctions among people. Mark goes out of his way to show how the kingdom touches and changes the lives of women as well as men. Distinctions once made on the basis of gender are not appropriate in the kingdom of God. The last section challenged distinctions based on race. Again, the kingdom has no room for such distinctions. In love, God regards all people equally. Mark is asking us to look at how we hold those kinds of distinctions in our hearts and how they play out in our lives.

The demands of the kingdom are great, but so are its promises. "The amount you measure out is the amount you will be given…and more besides."

Key Points for Preaching

The central issue facing the preacher and the congregation in this section of the gospel is again the choice between two worlds. But the preacher can examine this issue from new angles, and can call on us to explore a number of issues that might influence that choice. Material things may weigh our freedom down. Fear, especially the fear of death, may paralyze us. We may be wary of the strangers Jesus wants us to welcome into our circle. And perhaps most insidiously, the gospel may have just become too familiar, rather than a claim that shakes our familiar world to its foundations.

Using the story of the death of John the Baptist, the preacher has a chance to raise the question of death and eternal life. He or she can go beyond notions of eternal life as a reward that lasts through endless time and reflect on Rahner's theme of how we shape our eternal reality even now as we cooperate with the grace of God in this life. John shaped a self anchored in fidelity, radical honesty, and a willingness to sacrifice. How are we shaping ourselves for all eternity in the everyday patterns of our lives?

The preacher also has the chance to explore the notion that discipl ship is not a private matter. We were not baptized for the sake of our salvation alone. We were baptized so that our lives might proclaim the message of the gospel. Mark tells us in this section that the power that Jesus won in conquering Satan has been given to us. The homilist might ask in what ways we claim that power and use it for the sake of others.

CHAPTER SEVEN

BREAD AND THE GENTILES

Mark 6:30–8:33

Wisdom has built her house,
　　she has set up her seven columns;
She has dressed her meat, mixed her wine,
　　yes, she has spread her table.
She has sent out her maidens; she calls
　　from the heights out over the city:
"Let whoever is simple turn in here;
　　to him who lacks understanding, I say,
Come, eat of my food,
　　and drink of the wine I have mixed!
Forsake foolishness that you may live;
　　advance in the way of understanding."

Proverbs 9:1–6 (NAB)

The World of the Text

The return of the disciples from their missionary journey in 6:30 opens a section of the gospel dealing with several important issues in Mark The theme of bread looms large not only in the two miracles of th loaves but also in the many subtle references to bread throughout section. Mark also argues to its conclusion the question of the ac

C. The Third Cycle
1. What to do with bread: the second miracle of the loaves.
2. The struggle to understand the bread: the yeast of the Pharisees.
3. Miracle: the healing of a blind man.

As usual, Mark begins his retelling of the first miracle of the loaves with a reference to Jesus' teaching without mentioning the content of the teaching. This time, however, Mark places even more weight on Jesus' teaching by emphasizing his compassion for the people and by contrasting Jesus' care for the crowds with the neglect of the people by the religious leaders. With the words "for they were like sheep without a shepherd," Mark echoes the diatribe of the prophet Ezekiel against the leadership of ancient Israel in Ezekiel 34. The teaching here lies in the miracle of the loaves and fishes itself, and with this emphatic introduction Mark notes its importance to the gospel as a whole.

The miracle also takes place in the context of the return of the disciples from their missionary journey. The contrast between the disciples and the Jewish leadership in chapter three finds an echo here. The disciples are not to imitate the religious leadership of the scribes and Pharisees. The compassion and care that Jesus shows the people comprise the true model of religious leadership in the community of Jesus.

The themes of chapter four resound even more clearly in this miracle. The parables of chapter four concentrated on seeds and the great yield of grain the seeds could produce. Chapter four also contained the short warning that how one measures out now will determine how it will be measured back later. Here we see both the parables and that saying in action. The disciples are called upon to share what little they have, and in doing so they find that what they have is multiplied beyond their expectations. The small seed they plant by sharing the five loaves and two fish becomes enough to feed the large crowd. Here then is an example of what trusting in the promises of the kingdom means in the concrete. In this situation faith calls for sharing one's food. When they do that, they realize the promise that in the kingdom God will provide for his people. The disciples have more food after they share what they have than they had when the miracle story began. How they measure out what they have is how God measures out for their sake.

the first section of the gospel, the deep hopes humanity has had from the beginning of time. Participation in the banquet of the kingdom of God brings this century-old longing to its fulfillment.

It is not only the Jewish people who have had such longings. The first chapter of Mark speaks to the longings in the hearts of the whole human race. The banquet is meant for all peoples. Thus Mark recalls the story of the first multiplication of loaves, which took place in Jewish territory, with a similar story in Gentile territory in 8:1–9. The journeys of Jesus' ministry bring alienated peoples together in the name of the kingdom.

The major themes present in the second story of the loaves and fish are much the same as those in the first miracle: something small is turned into something great when it is given for the sake of others; God satisfies the hunger of his people with bread in the wilderness, a place of the new beginnings of the kingdom. The story bears the overtones of the celebration of the Eucharist. The one major difference is that this miracle takes place for the sake of the Gentiles. Mark continues his pattern of parallel miracles in Jewish and Gentile territories and so continues to emphasize his theme of the inclusion of the Gentiles in the Christian community and Eucharist. He highlights the Gentile character of this miracle with the number seven, the number of loaves and the number of baskets recovered. Seven could stand for the Gentile mission to the seventy nations and the seven deacons the early church chose to serve the widows of Greek-speaking Jews. It could also simply be the number recognized by all ancient peoples as the number of fullness and completion. Mark also notes that this crowd had been with Jesus for three days before this miracle of the kingdom took place. The reader could take that as a very subtle reference to the fullness of the kingdom realized after Jesus' three days in the tomb.

The bread miracles encapsulate many of the key themes of the gospel. The stories that follow them, the second element in each of the three sequences, ask how well the followers of Jesus are handling these themes. Mark paints a picture of their profound struggle to come to terms with the gospel and the mystery that it holds.

The first of these stories in 6:45–52 finds the disciples alone on the lake late in the day. Evening is coming on. Jesus had sent them ahead while he dismissed the five thousand whom they had fed in the first miracle of the loaves. The fact that they are without Jesus emphasizes Mark's point that Jesus is preparing them to take over the mission of the gospel after his death and resurrection. How are they faring without him? Not well.

This is the second encounter with Jesus in the midst of danger on the seas. The first such encounter took place after the discourse in chapter four. There the disciples became afraid in the midst of a storm, and Jesus, after quieting the storm, rebuked the Twelve and asked them if they had any faith. Here in chapter six the disciples again find themselves in trouble, this time because the wind is against them. However, Jesus is not with them. He has stayed behind on the shore to pray. This story, then, emphasizes the theme, first developed in chapter six, of the time when the disciples will be on their own. There will come a time when Jesus will no longer be with them because of his death and resurrection. Their mission began well earlier in the chapter, but the story of the beheading of John the Baptist raised the note of opposition to the gospel. They are tiring and once again they are struggling at sea. This is not the terrible storm of chapter four, but the winds are against them. The theme of the chaos that disciples must face in conversion to the gospel lurks under the surface of this story.

In the midst of their struggle Jesus approaches them, walking on the water. The symbolism here is rich. As we have seen, water represents the chaos that God had to tame in creating the world (Gn 1:2, 6–10), in freeing his people (Ex 14–15), and in defeating the evil that threatened Israel (Is 51:9–10). The theme is also found in Job 9:8, "(God) alone stretched out the heavens and trampled the waves of the Sea," and Job 38:16, "Have you entered into the springs of the sea, or walked in the recesses of the deep?" In Jesus God once again trods on God's ancient foe and brings peace and calm to his struggling people. But the disciples' response to all this is fear. Mark points out that their fear is a product of their inability to understand. Their minds are closed. Then Mark says something that ought to focus our attention on this section of the gospel: they failed to understand the miracle of the loaves. In the midst of opposition and danger they did not understand what they were to do with bread. They were completely dumbfounded.

A second story dealing with the struggle to understand what must be done with bread follows the second miracle of the loaves in 8:11–21. This one also takes place in the boat on the sea. It is triggered, however, by a discussion with the Pharisees in which they test him by asking for a sign from heaven to demonstrate his authority. Jesus says that no such sign will be given. In fact there have been signs in abundance as the kingdom has been manifested in his ministry. The question is whether one has the sight and hearing that are needed to perceive the signs and so come to faith. Mark again emphasizes that the religious leadership of his time is unable to perceive the work of God and is therefore deficient.

Having refused the request for a sign, Jesus gets back in the boat, which has served as a symbol to link the Jews and Gentiles in the ministry of Jesus and his disciples. Once they are in the boat, they deal with the real issue, bread. The following strange discussion ensues:

> They had forgotten to bring bread, and they had only one loaf with them in the boat. He enjoined them, "Watch out, guard against the leaven of the Pharisees and the leaven of Herod." They concluded among themselves that it was because they had no bread. When he became aware of this he said to them, "Why do you conclude that it is because you have no bread? Do you not yet understand or comprehend? Are your hearts hardened? Do you have eyes and not see, ears and not hear? And do you not remember, when I broke the five loaves for the five thousand, how many wicker baskets full of fragments you picked up?" They answered him, "Twelve." "When I broke the seven loaves for the four thousand, how many full baskets of fragments did you pick up?" They answered (him), "Seven." He said to them, "Do you still not understand?" (Mk 8:14–21, NAB)

Again the disciples do not understand what is going on with bread. They assume they have none, and thus they have nothing with which to feed the hungry masses. Yet Mark cryptically remarks that they had forgotten to take bread with them and that they had but one loaf in the boat. Obviously the one loaf they have to give that is with them in the boat, going unrecognized, is Jesus. They do have something to feed the masses, something that can grow miraculously, but they don't understand it. Jesus then rebukes them strongly, tying together two important themes as he does so. First, he asks them about their ability to perceive. Do they have eyes that cannot see and ears that cannot hear? This direct reference to his quotation from Isaiah in Mark 4:13 explains why the mystery is so difficult to solve for those on the outside. In fact, the disciples have the same problems of perception as those on the outside. Furthermore, he has them recall the two miracles of the loaves.

It all has to do with bread. A strong case can be made that what the disciples are struggling to understand is threefold. First, despite opposition and apparently dim prospects, God is able to bring about his promises. God was able to feed great multitudes with very little. Therefore the disciples must come to see and trust that the promises of the kingdom are real possibilities if they will only have faith in them. Secondly, they are struggling with the reason why they were called upon to distribute the loaves to others in need. Discipleship means serving others by sharing the very stuff of our lives. The reality of the kingdom grows by being given away to others. The disciples must plant the seeds of the kingdom for the sake of the harvest. They must give the stuff of their own lives, their former jobs, their kinship ties, and their own food to feed the hunger of others. With the death of John the Baptist even their own lives might be the seeds they will be called on to give for the sake of the harvest of the kingdom. When they sow the seed of the kingdom in this way, they have to trust it to produce miraculous harvests. Finally, the disciples are struggling with the issue of the inclusion of the Gentiles. This is stretching their preconceived notions of the kingdom, and they are finding it difficult to understand.

The middle or B cycle of this section of the gospel also tells stories of what to do with bread and the disciples' struggle to understand what they are doing. This cycle, however, points to the issue of the Gentiles as a central cause of a lack of understanding and chaos in the disciples' lives. It is one of those passages in the gospel in which Jesus speaks directly to an issue that was tearing at the fabric of Mark's community: the role of the Law in their communal life.

Mark 7:1–23 serves as the second cycle's story about what to do with bread. It involves a long discussion about the meaning of the law. Mark primarily aims the discussion at issues of eating and table fellowship: what constitutes ritual cleanliness for eating at table? The Pharisees' objection to the disciples of Jesus eating bread without washing their hands touches off the argument. Many English translations fail to catch what is clearer in the Greek: that the problem has to do with how they eat their bread. Bread remains the issue. Mark notes how the Pharisees and all the Jews do not eat without washing and that they also are careful to observe the proper rituals in the washing of dishes. The Pharisees claim that Jesus and his disciples have no respect for the traditions of their people. Themes from sections two and three of the gospel echo loudly here. Detractors made the same accusation against the disciples of Jesus when they picked grain on the Sabbath (2:23–28). And the Jewish leadership dismissed Jesus' whole movement as the work of Satan in 3:2–27.

Jesus responds by stating what it truly means to honor the traditions of their people. The Pharisees may be good in such matters as the washing of hands and dishes, but they ignore the weightier matters of the Law. Jesus points out how they have found legal ways around the obligation to honor and care for one's parents. Jesus then gets to the heart of the matter with his proclamation on what makes a person clean or unclean in 7:13–23. It is not how one eats but the deeds that come from a person that make him or her clean or unclean. Again, the passage recalls earlier stories. The woman with the hemorrhage and the leper from chapter one both raised issues of ritual purity. Jesus dealt with them as if they were clean in his eyes and the eyes of God. Now the issue of their cleanliness has come center stage. Jesus proclaims that disease or how one eats do not defile a person. How people deal with others in their actions makes them clean or unclean.

The first level of meaning of the passage is fairly obvious. Jesus defines ritual cleanliness to be a matter of the heart and of one's intentions. It no longer simply involves what foods one eats and how one prepares to eat them. Thus Mark can claim in 7:19 that Jesus had pronounced all foods clean. Mark ridicules the outward observance of the Pharisees that has no correlation with what is in their hearts and minds. He claims they actually set the intention of law aside, while keeping the insignificant details. Mark again finds the religious leadership of the Pharisees and Scribes wanting. He clearly wishes his community to concentrate on the matters of the heart and not simply on outward observances. Here Mark is further developing the significance of the confrontations of chapter two where Jesus set aside the Sabbath law and declared that the new reality of the kingdom could not be forced into the patterns of the old law. New wine cannot be put in old wineskins.

This passage bears other implications beyond how Mark interprets the meaning of the Torah for his community. If the regulations regarding ritual purity are now a matter of the heart and not of ritual washings, then the table fellowship of the Christian community is open to those to whom it had been closed by a strict following of the Torah. Mark is arguing that Gentiles are now welcome at the table of Jewish Christians because the reality of the kingdom has set aside the rules regarding ritual purity. If we were to glance behind the text and hazard a guess at what situation Jesus is speaking about in the community for which Mark is writing his gospel, I would guess it was an early Christian potluck gone bad.

Mark's community was a mixture of Jewish and Gentile converts. One of the Gentile women brought her best ham for the community to share. The Jewish Christians were aghast at the prospect of eating non-kosher food and were wondering what to do. Jesus gives a simple answer in this passage: you eat the ham. The relations among the community members are more important for living in the kingdom of God than laws regarding ritual purity. The issue may have involved more than the eating of non-kosher food at a potluck, however. The argument in Mark's community may have centered on the sharing of Eucharist with those considered unclean. Mark would then clearly be saying that the Eucharist is meant for all those who have placed their faith in the kingdom, Gentile and Jew. The Eucharist brings people together in the kingdom; it does not divide. Mark's community may have been struggling with the issue of whether Jews and Gentiles could share meals and Eucharist together. It was an issue in the early Church and can also be seen in the developments of Acts 10—15. Mark's position is clear: you cannot put new wine in old wineskins.

The story of the struggle to understand what we are to do with bread in this B cycle shows us Jesus himself grappling with the issue. In 7:24–30 Jesus has moved with his disciples into Gentile territory around the city of Tyre. There a Canaanite woman asks him to cast a demon out of her daughter. Jesus responds with a metaphor using bread. In the Greek it is the bread of the children that must not be given to the puppies. With courage reminiscent of the Jewish woman with the hemorrhage, the Canaanite woman replies that even the puppies get crumbs that fall from the table. Jesus recognizes her claim on the kingdom of God and casts out the demon. Mark pictures Jesus himself struggling with the fact of the prior claim of the Jewish people on the reality of the kingdom but then recognizing that its promises are for all people. Old ways of thinking cannot contain the reality of the kingdom.

As all of this struggle takes place in the hearts of disciples and between various groups in the time of Jesus and that of the Markan community, the kingdom continues to take root as it changes people's lives. The third element in each of the three cycles of this section of the gospel shows the kingdom manifest in miracles. In the first of these stories (6:53–56), Jesus and his disciples have completed the crossing after the story of Jesus' walking on the water. The crossing should place them in Gentile territory, for they have just left the scene of the miracle of the loaves for the five thousand. They meant to cross to Bethsaida, but Mark says they landed at Gennesaret. Gennesaret lies on the northwest coast of the Sea of Galilee. Thus the crossing took them back to a spot that was fairly close to their departure point. The wind may have blown them off course, but what we are dealing with in this story is something in the world of the Markan text that can be confusing: the journeys of Jesus do not always make geographical sense.

Mark may not have had a very good knowledge of the geography of Palestine, or he may not have paid close attention to how the geography played out as he rearranged the stories he found in the tradition in order to meet the theological needs of the gospel. The latter is probably more likely because places tend to play more of a theological role than a geographical one in Mark's gospel. What has probably happened is that 6:45 was followed in the tradition by the healing of the blind man in 8:22ff. Mark had reasons for moving the healing of the blind man toward the end of chapter eight in order to use it to introduce the next section of the gospel. Thus the geographical problem may be the result of Mark's redaction of the traditional materials.

The problem involves more than geography, however. Mark 6:53–56 is another Markan summary like those we found in 1:32–34 and 3:7–12. Both of those summary actions took place in Jewish territory.

Does Mark intend this summary to take place in Gentile territory and so maintain the balance between the work of the kingdom among the Jews and the Gentiles? If it takes place in Bethsaida, Mark places it in Gentile territory and so maintains the balance. If it takes place in Gennesaret, Jesus is in Jewish territory, in which case this is not an instance of Mark's using his material to develop his position on the Gentile issue. The text reads as if the events summarized took place in Gennesaret; therefore, the weight of the argument must be against a Gentile setting for the miracles. However, the context would argue the opposite. The disciples have just crossed the sea, which Mark usually uses as a transition between Jewish and Gentile territory. Further, the passage comes just before a long section dealing primarily with the Gentile question. Finally, one might ask why Mark included another summary at this point of the gospel. The inclusion of the Gentiles in the miracles of the kingdom would provide the best reason to do so.

The second cycle of this section ends with the healing of the deaf man in 7:31–37. This is another miracle that takes place in Gentile territory, showing that the Gentiles can share in the harvest of the kingdom. Geography again becomes confusing in 7:31. Jesus leaves Tyre to return to Galilee, but he does so by traveling north toward Sidon, which is in the opposite direction from Galilee. In doing so, Jesus somehow winds up east of his destination in the region of the Decapolis. Mark is either very confused or is trying to emphasize the fact that Jesus is spending a fair amount of time in Gentile territory.

At one level this healing of the deaf man serves to show the power of the kingdom as it continues to grow in spite of the opposition and chaos that threaten it. Another dimension to this miracle emerges, however: Jesus performs this healing in two steps. First there is the touching of the parts of the body that are in need of healing and then the command to be opened. This miracle is the first of two miracles in Mark's gospel that are carried out in this two–step fashion. The second takes place in chapter eight and involves the healing of a blind man. The fact that both miracles involve two steps calls attention to them and draws them together. Most importantly, the ailments they heal concern a central theological problem in this section of the gospel: seeing and hearing. In 4:12 Mark had stated that it was blindness and deafness that were keeping people from faith in the kingdom of God. In 7:14–21 he asks whether the disciples are failing to hear and see. Now as a crucial section of the gospel approaches, Mark shows his readers that even this lack of perception can be healed and that faith is possible if we will just continue the gospel journey. The disciples may not have all the answers. They may continue to struggle with chaos in their hearts and minds as they are converted from one world of meaning to another. But if they have faith and continue the journey with Jesus, if they trust the seed enough to plant it and let it grow, if they believe the bread they have can feed thousands, the kingdom will come.

The third cycle of this section of the gospel closes with the healing of a blind man in 8:22–26. Like the healing of the deaf man this miracle involves two steps. Jesus first puts spittle on the man's eyes and asks if he can see. His sight is restored, but things are very blurry. People look like trees walking about. Jesus then lays his hands on the man's eyes and his sight is restored. Four things stand out in this healing. First, like the other miracles of this section of the gospel, it closes one of the section's three cycles with a manifestation of the power of the kingdom. Secondly, if seeing and hearing correctly are an issue in the gospel, this miracle speaks powerfully of the kingdom's capacity to heal blindness and deafness. If disciples have trouble recognizing the new world of the kingdom of God, they will receive perception if they risk following Jesus. Thirdly, this passage and the healing of the deaf man are two-step miracles. Perception comes slowly. In this section Mark pictures the disciples struggling mightily to see in order to understand. They will eventually be healed. Discipleship is a journey that involves growth over time, not a sudden change. Finally, this last miracle has no formal closure. The proper form for a miracle story involves some acclamation or amazement in response to what Jesus and the kingdom have brought to those with faith. This story lacks this concluding element. It leaves us hanging, looking to the next section of the gospel for this final element. Mark will not disappoint us.

Reflections in Front of the Text

What are we to do with bread? Christians know that they are to bring it to the altar and in some mysterious way God transforms it into the body of God's Son, Jesus. There is more to bread than immediately meets the eye, but can we see what is possible with bread?

The problem for many Christians is that this Eucharistic transformation of bread takes place up on the altar. What this miracle says about the rest of our lives beyond the altar is hard to see. But Mark provides clue after clue in this section of his gospel to help us understand not only what is possible with bread, but also what is possible with life. Simply laying bread on the altar and saying the proper words are not enough to give us the fullness of what God intends in the Eucharist. We must break the bread and share it. Christ is not present in the Eucharist simply for the sake of being there. Jesus is in our midst for the sake of action.

Bread is symbolic. It stands for the whole of the life that it nourishes. It symbolizes all we have and are. Under the sign of bread we place our lives on the altar, and that is what is changed into the Body of Christ. The miraculous transformation does not take place on the altar alone. God changes the whole substance of our lives in the Eucharist. But it is not enough simply to place ourselves on the altar. We must be broken and shared. The act that is performed symbolically in the Eucharist and lived daily in discipleship makes Christ present in the world.

We have been given the stuff of life not only for our own sake but also for the sake of others. We are to use what we have in life in the service of others. Even our baptism into Christ was not merely for our own salvation, but that Christ might enter the world again through us for the salvation of others. We are the Body of Christ.

It is not easy to see these things. The way of being in the world that stands over against the kingdom is a world in which the self comes first. Greed is a virtue in an economic system that sees only scarcity in life. Such a world hoards its bread.

Disciples of Jesus must see five things clearly as they contemplate the mystery of the kingdom in this section of the gospel. First of all, discipleship involves serving others with what God has given us. Jesus tells his disciples to feed the five thousand even though they seem to have scarcely anything themselves. Whatever a disciple has, it is to be used in service.

Secondly, we must trust that the bread we give for the sake of others will be enough. Like the seeds of the fourth section of the gospel, it will grow and be enough for all. The economics of the kingdom of God are an economics of plenty rather than of scarcity. The kingdom will grow and God will provide if we but plant the seeds of what we have. Something other than the world we are used to is possible for human life.

Thirdly, the banquet of the kingdom includes all. In this section Mark stares hard into the face of the greatest prejudice the early church faced, the great wall that separated Jew from Gentile. Mark tells us that such walls must come down because God has invited all peoples to the banquet of the kingdom. We cannot put new wine into old wineskins. The divisions that marked the human geography of the old world cannot stand in the new world of God's kingdom. Racial prejudices, sexism, distinctions based on class and income are not valid in the world God offers to us. We must leave that old world behind to enter the promises of God's kingdom.

Fourthly, all of this is eucharistic. To break the very stuff of life and share it with others is the act that God uses to transform bread and human life into the presence of God's Son, Jesus. What happens at the altar mirrors what God is doing throughout the whole of our lives.

Finally, Mark has moved us very close to the heart of the mystery of the kingdom in this section. The secret of the kingdom, so hard to solve, is actually quite simple. The kingdom comes about when Jesus and his disciples give it to one another. We do not simply receive it from God. We receive it from God through one another. The kingdom will not come unless we give it to one another. The promises we hold so dearly in our hearts in the first section of the gospel are realities we must bestow on each other.

Oddly, for Mark all of this is not a matter of mere doing. It is a matter of seeing reality correctly. If we learn to see things properly, right action will follow. Mark writes his gospel to help us to see so that the mystery of the kingdom might be broken open.

Key Points for Preaching

The miracles of the loaves serve as the centerpieces of this section of the gospel. The homilist would do well to keep them in mind when considering any of the stories that make up this part of the gospel. Those miracle stories encourage us first to reflect on what it is we are to do with the stuff of our lives. By stuff I mean not only the possessions we have, possessions which can encumber our lives, but also the very life and energy we have and are.

Mark invites us to contemplate the fact that if we use the stuff of our lives for the sake of feeding others, life begins to grow in ways beyond our expectations. Just as in the last section we saw that our baptism was not for our own sake alone, but also for the sake of others, so in this section Mark tells us that our lives are not for our sake alone but have been given to us so that we might give life to others. We can do this by simply feeding others the food they need to survive. But we can also use our energy, our talents, even our professions and jobs to serve others. The miracle of the loaves promises that the stuff of our lives grows in the giving.

This section of the gospel also invites us to contemplate the role of law in our lives. For many people religion is a matter of law. It involves keeping the commandments and all the rules and regulations that are so much a part of church life. There is a place for all this, but Mark tells us that the Law is not ultimate. The kingdom of God comes first. All other matters will find their proper place when the focus is kept clearly on the kingdom.

The preacher can also consider the theme of inclusion and exclusion. Our rules and patterns of life often exclude others. The gospel demands that we look at such exclusions with a critical eye. In fact, the gospel almost reaches the point of humor when it talks about the washing of hands and dishes as key elements of religious practice and a reason for the exclusion or discipline of some of God's people. Inclusion is the fundamental rule of the kingdom of God.

Most importantly, this section gives the homilist a chance to reflect upon the Eucharist and its connections with the rest of our lives. Mark first approaches Eucharistic themes by telling stories of feeding people who are hungry. Far too often we think of the Eucharist in terms of the real presence of Jesus in the bread and wine and forget that Jesus is present not just to be there but to do something. Action takes place around the altar, but it also needs to spread beyond the altar and reshape the rest of our lives into the pattern of the Eucharist. Mark tells us that the fundamental pattern of the Eucharist is feeding one another with the basic stuff of life, bread. It is not just the bread and wine that are made into the body and blood of Jesus. We are also transformed. God transforms us as we pray the eucharistic prayer and offer the sacrifice of Jesus. We are the body of Christ when we use our lives to serve others.

CHAPTER EIGHT

BLINDNESS AND THE CROSS

Mark 8:22–10:52

Do you not know that all of us who have been baptized into Christ
Jesus were baptized into his death? Therefore we have been buried
with him by baptism into death, so that, just as Christ was raised from
the dead by the glory of the Father, so we too might walk in newness
of life. For if we have been united with him in a death like his, we will
certainly be united with him in a resurrection like his. We know that
our old self was crucified with him so that the body of sin might be
destroyed, and we might no longer be enslaved to sin. For whoever has
died is freed from sin. But if we have died with Christ, we believe that
we will also live with him.

Romans 6:3–8 (NRSV)

The World of the Text

In the previous section the symbol of bread took Mark's readers close to
the heart of the mystery of the gospel. Mark told us that we embrace the
kingdom in faith by the way we use bread, which represents the very stuff
of our lives. If we give it away for the sake of others, the promises of the
kingdom flourish. In this next section, 8:22—10:52, Mark speaks more
plainly. He finally informs us that the centerpiece of the mystery of the

kingdom is the cross. Three times he tells us of Jesus predicting his passion, death, and resurrection, and inviting his disciples to follow him
along that path. The Markan Jesus claims that it is the only way to the
fullness of life that God has promised his people. But the question of
perception continues to haunt the gospel even in the midst of such plain
speaking. We find the disciples continuing to struggle to see and hear
properly throughout the whole of this, the eighth, section of the gospel.

Two themes dominate the structure of Mark 8:22—10:52: the proclamation of the cross and the question of whether disciples can grasp how
and why the cross is central to the realization of the kingdom. The issue
of the struggle for insight into the nature of the kingdom is not new.
Mark has prepared his reader for it in the previous section with the twin
two-step miracles, the healing of a deaf man in 7:31–37 and the healing
of a blind man in 8:22–26. This question of seeing and hearing properly also repeats themes present throughout the gospel. Just before the
cure of the blind man, Jesus questions the disciples about whether they
are able to perceive or not. In 8:18 he finally asks them, "Do you have
eyes that do not see, ears that do not hear?" This quotation from Isaiah
echoes the more extended use of the quotation in chapter four where
Jesus explains that people are taught in parables precisely "so that they
may see and see again, but not perceive; may hear and hear again, but
not understand." The question of accurate perception extends even as
far back as chapter two and causes us to ask why the opposition to Jesus
is developing there. It may not be so much a question of evil intention
as of the inability of the Jewish leaders to perceive and understand what
is taking place within their midst.

In the eighth section Mark emphasizes the question of seeing and
hearing properly by enclosing the whole section with two stories of the
healing of blind men. The story of the healing of the blind man in
8:22–26 not only closes the last section but also serves as a hinge, intro-
ducing the eighth section of the gospel. Mark ends the eighth section in
10:46–52 with the healing of another blind man. Professions of Jesus'
identity follow both of these healings. In 8:29 Peter professes that Jesus
is the Messiah. This is accurate but incomplete. Like the blind man in
8:24, Peter can see, but things are still a bit blurry. Jesus will have to
push Peter and the other disciples further into the mystery through his

predictions of the passion, and through the reflections on discipleship that accompany the passion predictions. The second blind man in Mark 10:46–52 can see. He professes that Jesus is the Messiah by giving him the Messianic title, Son of David. But unlike Peter, the cured blind man sees what this implies. He makes his real profession of faith by following Jesus along the way. His sight enables him to follow Jesus along the road that leads to the cross. Throughout the section Mark depicts the disciples of Jesus struggling to understand what Jesus is trying to teach them. Their failure to see things clearly causes them to stumble on the path down which he is leading them. The whole section leads from Peter's blurred vision to the clarity of someone who can see that discipleship involves following Jesus to the cross.

The second major theme consists of the object of clear seeing and hearing: the message of the cross. Mark structures this section to emphasize the cross and explain its implications for discipleship. He repeats a basic narrative cycle centered on three predictions of the passion. This structure both highlights the death and resurrection by reiteration and makes room for comment on what the cross means. The elements of this threefold cycle are the following:

- Jesus predicts the passion and resurrection;

- The disciples fail to understand;

- Jesus instructs his followers about discipleship;

- Jesus demonstrates his power as something that goes beyond normal expectations.

After the second cycle of stories Mark breaks open his threefold pattern to address a number of issues that seem to have been important to his first-century community. All those issues share the common theme of the difficulty of the path of discipleship. The overall structure of this section, then, looks like this:

Introduction: The healing of the first blind man and Peter's proclamation of Jesus' identity.

The First Cycle
  The prediction of the passion
  The disciples fail to understand

Jesus' instruction about discipleship as taking up the cross
Demonstrations of the power of the kingdom
> The transfiguration of Jesus
> The exorcism of a young boy

The Second Cycle
> The prediction of the passion
> The disciples fail to understand
> Jesus' instruction about discipleship as service
> The power of the kingdom beyond the inner circle
>> Issue of discipleship in the Markan community
>>> Leading others astray
>>> Divorce
>>> Children
>>> Riches

The Third Cycle
> The prediction of the passion
> The disciples fail to understand
> Jesus' instruction about discipleship
> The healing of the blind man at Jericho and his profession of
> faith in following Jesus.

Mark fills his gospel with characters who from a literary point of view are quite flat. They make quick appearances and are not developed in any depth because they simply serve as examples of a type of response to Jesus. Those who are able to see are those who respond with faith. Among them are the many people who have been healed by Jesus. They perceive the action of Jesus as the entry of God's kingdom into human life. They open their hearts to that reality, and the kingdom flourishes in their lives. Other figures like Simon of Cyrene (15:21) and the poor widow in the temple (12:41–44) have understood the central message of the kingdom. Simon will take up the cross and follow Jesus. That is exactly what discipleship calls for. The widow will put all the money she has into the temple treasury, a sign that all she has is at God's disposal. She sees that discipleship demands all that she has and is.

On the other hand, Mark's gospel depicts those flat characters that are not able to see. The Pharisees and scribes serve as primary examples of these types. They see Jesus as a heretic and one who breaks the law. They do not see the kingdom of God breaking into human affairs through the ministry of Jesus. Jesus' family also fails to appreciate him fully. They think of him as an upstart who has gone mad (3:20–21) and wonder where he has gotten his authority and power (6:1–6). Jesus is not able to work miracles among them because they have no faith. To have faith is to see clearly.

Such flat characters hardly depict the true struggle of discipleship, however. They simply demonstrate various types of responses to Jesus. Mark develops the character of the Twelve more fully in order to clarify the struggle and the journey involved in seeing properly and having faith. In chapter one they leave everything and follow Jesus. In chapter six they share the power and authority of Jesus on their first missionary journey. However, in chapter four they needed the parables explained to them, and they were frightened and without faith during the storm at sea. In chapter six they were again frightened and their minds were closed when they met Jesus walking on the water. They had not seen the meaning of the miracle of the loaves. Again in chapter eight Jesus asks them if they lack perception because they do not seem to have understood the meaning of the miracles of the loaves.

The disciples, therefore, are more fully realized characters, and their experiences represent a more realistic picture of the struggle of faith. Mark depicts discipleship as a difficult journey, and at the heart of the difficulty lies the issue of perceiving correctly. In contrast to Mark, the issue of discipleship in Matthew's gospel does not center on perception. Anyone can recognize Jesus and cry out "Lord, Lord" (Mt. 7:21–23). The question for Matthew is whether people will act on their faith. Mark pushes the issue more deeply and notes that a large part of the problem of discipleship is to see and hear things correctly. Faith and discipleship, he maintains, will flow from accurate perception.

The journey may be difficult, but Mark gives his readers hope by opening and closing this section of the gospel with the healing of blind men. These miracles show that it is possible to see properly and follow Jesus. The first of these healings, in 8:22–26, is difficult, for it takes Jesus two steps to heal the man. But eventually healing does take place. However, the healing of the blind man in chapter eight is not a complete miracle story. The standard element of awe and praise on the part of those who witness this great action of God is missing. This forces the reader to look to the next story for this element, and there one finds Peter providing the acclamation that completes the miracle story. Thus Mark closely ties Peter's proclamation that Jesus is the Messiah in 8:27–30 to the healing of the blind man. He depicts Peter as a man of faith who can see properly and name Jesus correctly.

But when we look at the more developed character of Peter, we see that the healing of spiritual blindness involves more than just proclaiming Jesus as Messiah. In the seventh section of the gospel the Twelve struggled to understand the mystery of the kingdom. Now Jesus heals Peter's spiritual blindness, and Peter is finally able to say that Jesus is the Messiah. With this statement of faith Peter recognizes that in Jesus God's kingdom is breaking into human life in a definitive way. He sees in the words and deeds of Jesus the ultimate action of God in human history. But is Peter's healing complete? Like the blind man in the previous story, Peter can see with the eyes of faith, but his vision still remains blurred. Peter struggles to understand Jesus' teaching on discipleship that follows his proclamation of faith. In 8:31–33 Jesus invites Peter and the disciples to see further and take another step on the journey of discipleship. Jesus ignores Peter's proclamation that he is the Messiah and instead refers to himself as the Son of Man. He then begins to tell his disciples about his impending execution and resurrection. Peter cannot grasp this, so he takes Jesus aside and tries to correct him, only to have Jesus correct him in turn.

The prediction of the passion finally lifts a veil, and we are now able to see clearly the great stumbling block that has kept so many people in the gospel from faith. Disciples of Jesus must come to terms with the cross, which has cast its shadow over the reality of the kingdom throughout the gospel. In this section of the gospel Mark concentrates his readers' attention on the cross and what the cross means for discipleship. Since Peter cannot accept that the Messiah must suffer an ignominious death, his vision remains blurred, like that of the blind man in the previous passage.

Jesus works hard to heal Peter and the rest of the Twelve by instructing them that discipleship requires self-renunciation, but that to lose one's life for the sake of the gospel is to gain life in its fullness. We see a paradox clearly expressed here which Mark has hinted at before in his gospel. Chapter four used parabolic images of seeds for the great Christian paradox that we must let go of our lives for the sake of the gospel in order to find life in its fullness. We must let go of seed so that it might be planted and produce a crop. We are called to measure things out generously and that is how life will be measured back to us. In chapter six the sharing of the little food one has with other hungry people and the miraculous meal that results provide a striking instance of the paradox of giving and finding life. Finally, in this section Jesus puts the basic Christian mystery clearly: to be his follower involves giving one's life for others and thereby finding the fullness of life in the kingdom. Twice Mark refers to the kingdom in this context, first via the image of the Son of Man returning in glory and secondly in Jesus' declaration that some of those standing there with him will not die before they *see* the kingdom. Mark has carefully chosen the verb in 9:1; they will see the kingdom.

In this first cycle the transfiguration demonstrates that this paradox has the power to bring the kingdom to reality. The transfiguration manifests Jesus' power beyond all expectations. This manifestation of Jesus in glory is tied closely with the baptism. In each incident the voice from heaven refers to Jesus as God's Son, and each of these crucial episodes gives the gospel special depth and direction.

Scholars have long discussed whether the transfiguration anticipates the resurrection of Jesus or the end-time appearance of the Son of Man in his glory in the kingdom. Those who argue that it is a resurrection appearance point to 9:9–10, where Jesus warns the three disciples not to tell what they have seen until after he has risen. They also point out that in the best manuscripts of Mark's gospel there are no resurrection appearances of Jesus. The best manuscripts end at 16:8 with the angel's instruction to go and meet Jesus in Galilee. Perhaps Mark has moved a resurrection appearance to this place in the gospel to encourage the reader who has just heard he has to die with Jesus in order to find life in the kingdom.

Other scholars, however, believe that the transfiguration manifests

Jesus in power in the kingdom at the end of time, and they cite the following evidence. First, they note the apocalyptic nature of the appearance: it takes place on a mountain; the garments are white, an apocalyptic color; the glory of God is present in the cloud; and Elijah, a figure closely tied to apocalyptic themes, is given precedence over Moses. (Matthew mentions Moses first and thus changes the emphasis of the appearance.) Secondly, Mark encloses the transfiguration with apocalyptic references. In 9:1 he tells the disciples that some of them will see the kingdom before they die. In 9:12–13 he places a discussion about Elijah, the figure who will come before the Lord brings the kingdom into being. Finally, throughout the whole gospel Mark centers his attention on the kingdom. He focuses on the coming of the end-time character of the kingdom rather than the resurrection.

In 1:15 Mark opens the gospel with the proclamation of the kingdom, and he keeps the reader's attention centered there throughout. He clearly expects the arrival of the kingdom soon. Both in 9:1 and 13:30 he states that the kingdom and the events preceding it will happen before his own generation passes away. The arrival of the kingdom, then, preoccupies the mind of Mark and his community. Mark clearly identifies the way of discipleship as the way to the kingdom. He does not think the resurrection is unimportant; in fact, Mark has three predictions of it in this section of the gospel. However, in Mark's view the resurrection serves as another step on the way to the real goal of the Christian journey, the kingdom.

Mark places the transfiguration at this point in the gospel to remind his readers that we must keep our eyes on the kingdom of God. We have just heard the difficult news not only of Jesus' death and resurrection, but of ours as well. Unless we keep that goal before us, we will not be able to do what is necessary to reach it. We will not be able to pay the high price needed to reach the kingdom, which is nothing less than the giving of our whole lives. By placing the transfiguration here, Mark points out that only by keeping our attention on the ultimate goal of Christian and human life will we be able to walk the journey of discipleship. Even though the message may be hard to hear and grasp, the voice from heaven commands the disciples to listen to Jesus.

Mark closes off the first cycle of this section with another demonstration of Jesus' power in 9:14–29. Jesus cures an epileptic child, a cure beyond the power of his disciples. In relating this story, Mark expands the miracle form to include a discussion of whether the Twelve had faith enough to carry out the miracle. When Jesus hears that the disciples could not cast out the demon that they presumed had caused the epileptic fits, he explodes with the words, "You faithless generation" (9:19). Later he adds, "All things can be done for the one who believes," and the father of the boy responds, "I believe; help my unbelief" (9:23–24). Thus Mark is able to close off the first cycle of this section with a strong emphasis on faith, the ability to see the meaning and the implications of Jesus' words and action. He is also able to end with an emphasis on prayer, which is the way one comes to see properly and keep one's eye on the kingdom throughout one's life. In spite of these visions and demonstrations of the power of the kingdom, the Twelve still struggle with faith, and therefore the kingdom has trouble emerging in their ministry and their lives.

The second cycle opens with the passion prediction in 9:30–32. It is the least detailed of the three passion predictions and therefore probably the most primitive. As Mark presents them, the passion predictions have been shaped in their detail by the early Church's memory of the actual events of Jesus' death and resurrection. The early traditions of the Church placed them, with all their anachronistic detail, on the lips of Jesus. If that is so, this second prediction, because of its simplicity, is probably from the oldest tradition. By placing it here Mark stresses again the central theme of his gospel: that the only way to the kingdom lies on the path that leads through the cross.

At the beginning of this second cycle Mark emphasizes that Jesus is avoiding the crowds because he is instructing his disciples in this core element of discipleship. The disciples, however, are not catching on. Chapter 9:32 explicitly states that they did not understand, and 9:33–34 shows that their concern about who will be the greatest in the kingdom manifests their lack of insight. Their struggle to see and believe continues. So Jesus again instructs them on the nature of discipleship.

An important shift takes place in this second cycle that allows Mark to explore more deeply the nature of discipleship. In the first cycle Jesus told the disciples that they must die and rise like him if they want to find life. The parallel to that instruction in the second cycle (9:33–37) accentuates the idea of service. Jesus asks the disciples what they were talking about on the road. When they give him no reply because they had been discussing which of them was the greatest, Jesus teaches them that the way to greatness in the kingdom of God lies through service to others. If you want to be great in the world of the kingdom, you must become the servant of all. When we do something as simple as welcoming a child, we welcome the Lord who comes bringing the kingdom in its fullness.

Jesus' equating the idea of service with the idea of death and resurrection in the first cycle gets at the heart of Mark's gospel. Every disciple must die and rise with the Lord. But not all do so in the same way. According to the early tradition of the church, all of the Twelve except John died a martyr's death. But many disciples gave their lives for the sake of others in daily service. That service need not be dramatic. It can be as simple as the care of a child. But Mark wants to make one thing clear in this section. A life given for the sake of others leads to fullness of life. That is the central mystery of the kingdom of God that is so difficult to understand in spite of the fact that it is so simple and is borne out in the experience of Jesus and those who follow him. The disciples struggle to understand this central mystery because it runs counter to the way that the world opposed to the kingdom sees reality. That false way glorifies self-promotion so that one may be recognized as the greatest. Those caught up in the kingdom of God see the dynamics of life very differently: how we measure out our lives for the sake of others determines how life in its fullness and greatness will be measured out to us.

The demonstration of Jesus' power in 9:38–40 confirms this teaching about discipleship. The power of Jesus' name works miracles and so brings about the kingdom even when the one using his name is not connected to Jesus in any obvious way. The boundaries of our imaginations cannot contain the power of the kingdom. If the entire world hungers for the kingdom Jesus brings (1:37), then who can claim to set up boundaries, especially institutional boundaries, around the power of that kingdom? All those who give their lives in service for others will experience the power of the kingdom of God working in their lives.

Mark then inserts into the second cycle of the passion predictions the discussion of a number of issues that must have been points of contention in the first-century Christian community. Doing so allows him to make specific pastoral applications of the gospel he proclaims. By placing these issues at this point in his narrative, he also uses them as examples of the radical call of discipleship. The notion of dying to self and finding new life with Jesus takes on particular significance when Mark's community deals with such issues as scandal and leading others away from the path of faith, divorce, the welcoming of children, and the possession of riches.

In looking at how Mark deals with these issues, two things must be kept in mind. First, Mark offers specific solutions to issues faced by the community for whom he wrote his gospel. He is not promulgating eternal doctrine. Secondly, one important issue looms on the horizon: Mark and his community were expecting the return of the Lord and the arrival of the kingdom in the near future. Therefore, he could call for a radical response of faith that overlooked or ignored temporal issues and responsibilities. Matthew, who came to recognize that the kingdom was not as near as Mark had thought, will offer different solutions to the same pastoral issues because his community will need practical advice about how to live out its Christian faith in an extended period of time before the kingdom arrives. Matthew has time for nuanced responses; Mark does not.

Chapter 9:42–50 concentrates on the issue of leading astray those who already have faith. In Mark Jesus exaggerates the imagery when he talks of cutting off hands and feet and plucking out one's eye rather than give scandal, but the point is clear: nothing should come between the disciple and the kingdom. The community must deal in a radical manner with anything that might get in the way of faith. They must value the kingdom above everything else. Mark places this instruction between the warning not to become an obstacle to others in 9:42 and the admonition to be at peace with one another in 9:50. Perhaps some in his community were taking to extremes the freedom of the Christian that Mark emphasized in chapter two and again in 7:1–23 and causing scandal. We could suppose that Mark was facing an issue similar to the one Paul addressed in 1 Corinthians 8–9. The Corinthians had been arguing whether Christians could eat meat that had been sacrificed to pagan idols. Some held that it was permissible because pagan sacrifice was nothing but an empty gesture. Others countered that eating such meat would give scandal to those who thought that such an act was a participation in the pagan ritual. Both Mark and Paul strongly emphasized the freedom of the Christian, but both tempered it by their concern for the spiritual welfare of others.

On the issue of divorce, Mark is strict. He does not allow divorce and remarriage in his community. Mark depicts Jesus holding this strict interpretation of the law. Jesus is not teaching something new. He is recalling a reality present from the beginning of human relationships. Jesus appeals to Genesis 1 as the basis of his interpretation of the Mosaic Law.

Mark's ruling on divorce and remarriage addresses a situation in which the community thought there was not much time at all left in human history. If the end of history and the arrival of the kingdom are near, the question of divorce and remarriage no longer takes on the same importance. One hardly has time to worry about the matter. The people of Matthew's community, however, realize that they will have time on their hands before the kingdom makes its final appearance. The pastoral situation differs from that of Mark, and Matthew makes allowance for that. He too forbids divorce and remarriage, but provides for pastoral discretion in 19:9. In the case of πορνεια (*porneia*) Matthew thinks there is room for divorce and remarriage. Christians still argue about what Matthew meant by πορνεια.

Another explanation for Mark's view of divorce may be that discipleship called for a radical renunciation of everything in the light of the approaching kingdom. Perhaps some in Mark's community were asking whether existing marriage relationships should be forsaken and husbands and wives left behind for the sake of the kingdom. If that was the issue, then Mark makes marriage an exception to the renunciations called for by the kingdom. The fact that spouses are not mentioned in the list of things left behind by disciples in 10:28–30 supports this reading.

The passage about the welcoming of children may be an example of the call of Christians to accept and cherish those who have no status in society. Such an interpretation fits well with Mark's insistence on the acceptance of outsiders and the rejected into the Christian community. This passage may also encourage the community to accept and care for its children and not abandon them to pursue the kingdom. However, Mark mentions children in 10:29 among those left behind for the sake of the kingdom. Perhaps the community cared for the children in common, or perhaps it was one's grown children who had to be left behind. In either case, while it is enticing to speculate about the issues the Markan community struggled with, our window into their world is cloudy at best. We need to remind ourselves that we are dealing in conjecture. Such a caution reminds us that they, like us, had to encounter life's harsh realities as they sought to understand what it meant to have faith and follow the way of Christian discipleship.

Mark then addresses the issue of wealth and again takes a position of radical renunciation. He views wealth as a major stumbling block to following the way of discipleship. He shows it graphically in the story of the aborted discipleship of a rich man in 10:17–22. The man wanted to follow Jesus, but his wealth got in the way. At that point Mark includes the sayings of Jesus that underscore how hard it is for the rich to enter the kingdom. Perhaps the Markan community called upon its members to renounce their wealth by giving it to the poor and then to center their attention on the kingdom. Such renunciation is easier if the kingdom is just around the corner. If it is delayed, some of the world's goods may be needed to maintain one's life and the life of the community. Matthew, recognizing a delay in the arrival of the kingdom, changes the story of the rich man to make room for pastoral discretion. In 19:16–22 Matthew makes a slight change in the text. He says that the total renunciation of one's goods is the way of perfection. He implies that it is not the only way into the kingdom. Others can be disciples without taking the extreme step of renouncing all their possessions. Matthew knows his community has to survive in time, and therefore it is not practical to give away all that they have. Mark, who is looking for the arrival of the kingdom in the near future, makes more radical demands. The kingdom makes far-reaching demands in both gospels, but the situations in which we find ourselves shape those demands.

In 10:28–30 the disciples again have trouble piecing all this together. Peter lists all that they have left behind and asks what is in store for them. Jesus answers that they will receive it all back in the kingdom and more. The great Christian paradox thus arises again. By giving of the substance of his life now, the fullness of life keeps coming back to the disciple. Jesus emphasizes the paradox even further by mentioning persecution among the experiences disciples can expect. The way to life in the kingdom lies only in the way of the cross. Finally, 10:31 closes the second cycle by mentioning again the paradoxical reversals that take place when one places one's life at the service of the kingdom. Those who are now last will be first in the kingdom.

The third cycle of this section of the gospel begins with the passion prediction in 10:32–34. Mark opens the cycle by pointing out that Jesus and the disciples were on the road, or on the way, going up to Jerusalem. Those introductory words sound a motif that has been playing quietly throughout this section of the gospel, the motif of the way. Since Peter's acclamation of faith at Caesarea Philippi in 8:27, Mark has depicted Jesus and the disciples slowly but surely making their way toward Jerusalem, where the crucifixion will take place. By the second passion prediction in 9:30 they have made their way back into Galilee. By 10:1 they have arrived in Judea and Transjordan. In 10:32 they find themselves on the road up to Jerusalem. And finally in 10:46 they are in Jericho, a short distance from Jerusalem. Beyond that Mark keeps reminding the reader that they are on the Way by his repetition of the Greek word ὁ ὁδοσ (*ho hodos*), which can be translated as "way" or "road", in 9:34, 10:32, and 10:52, and by his reference to the journey in 10:17. The whole movement of the gospel is now clearly directed toward Jerusalem and the cross as the only "Way" to the kingdom.

We must give credit to the disciples for continuing to follow Jesus in spite of where the Way is leading. They are men of faith, but their faith is still shaky and in need of growth. Chapter 10:32 depicts them as following Jesus as he walks on ahead of them, but they are in a daze and filled with apprehension. In this context Jesus makes his third prediction of his passion, death, and resurrection. But the disciples still cannot see the full mystery clearly. They do not yet fully understand that the road to the cross is the only road to life. Their faith must continue to grow.

The failure of the disciples to understand the meaning of the cross comes out clearly in 10:35–40. They are again concerned with positions of greatness in the kingdom. This time James and John, the sons of Zebedee, ask Jesus for key positions in the kingdom. A bit later the other ten are indignant at the presumption of their fellows. Jesus must again instruct them all that they will find greatness in the kingdom not through positions of power but through service. Jesus tells James and John that to enter the kingdom they must drink of the same cup that he, Jesus, must drink: the cross. Then he addresses the Twelve and emphasizes again that the only way to the kingdom is through service to others. Like the second cycle, this instruction on discipleship as service parallels the demand in the first cycle that disciples must follow Jesus on the way of the cross and be willing to give their lives for the kingdom. Giving life to others leads to life in the kingdom. The cross is the only way to the kingdom. The road that leads through wielding worldly power is a dead end.

Mark structures this section of the gospel to make his central claim about the mystery of the kingdom of God. In 8:34–38 we are told that the only way to life is the way of the cross, but Mark's readers are left to question what that might mean in our everyday lives. The parallels to 8:34–38 in 9:33–37,41 and 10:41–45 clearly spell out that the cross in daily life means service, and Christian service means pouring out one's life for others. If one wonders what the Christian way might mean, Mark states clearly that it involves service and that that service will make great demands upon us. We must come to see and understand the cross and the service it entails in order to embrace the kingdom of God. Resurrection and the kingdom come only through the cross. In 10:45 Jesus states clearly the main lesson of this section: "For the Son of Man himself did not come to be served but to serve, and to give his life as a ransom for many."

Finally, the healing of the blind man in 10:46–52 demonstrates Jesus' power yet again. This miracle and the other healing of a blind man in 8:22–26 enclose the whole section and raise the question whether one can properly see the central lesson of faith embodied here. The lesson is the cross. When this second blind man has been healed because of his faith, he follows Jesus along the Way. The last word in the section is the Greek word ʹοδοσ. When one can see properly, one walks with Jesus on the Way toward Jerusalem and the cross.

Reflections in Front of the Text

At the heart of the celebration of the Eucharist Christians keep coming back to the same theme, the death and resurrection of the Lord Jesus. The core of the eucharistic prayer repeats the theme again and again. In the second eucharistic prayer, for example, the celebrant introduces the words of consecration by saying, "Before he was given up to death, a death he freely accepted...." The words of consecration of the bread repeat the theme, "This is my body which will be given up for you." The consecration of the wine mentions it again, "This is the cup of my blood....It will be shed for you and for many." Then the presider invites the congregation to proclaim the mystery of our faith. Note that, like Mark in 4:11 ("To you is given the mystery of the kingdom of God"), the liturgy uses the singular, "mystery," in this context: "Let us proclaim the mystery of faith." The people proclaim one of four acclamations, each of them emphasizing death and resurrection:

Christ has died, Christ is risen, Christ will come again.

Dying you destroyed our death, rising you restored our life.
Lord Jesus come in glory.

When we eat this bread and drink this cup,
we proclaim your death, Lord Jesus, until you come in glory.

Lord, by your cross and resurrection you have set us free.
You are the savior of the world.

Finally at the high point of the liturgy the celebrant picks up the prayer again. Every eucharistic prayer highlights the same theme. The terse second eucharistic prayer runs as follows:

In memory of his death and resurrection,
We offer you, Father, this life giving bread, this saving cup.
We thank you for counting us worthy to stand in your presence
and serve you.

At the heart of the Eucharist, when we use bread for our most sacred act, we do exactly as Mark has bid us do in this section of the gospel. We join Jesus in his death and resurrection. We join him in giving our lives to God the Father, from whom they came in the first place.

For Jesus the cross and the resurrection were not isolated events. They were integrally related to the rest of his life and ministry. He gave his life for others on the cross just as he gave his life for others in his service to the kingdom of God. Every healing, every act of forgiveness, every exorcism, and every act of giving life in the ministry of Jesus expressed the same self–giving that was acted out so dramatically in the passion and death of the Lord. His death flowed out of his ministry. He was killed because he was faithful to the vision of reality that is the kingdom of God. He would not surrender to the world of the opposition, to the forces of darkness and oppression.

Our participation in the death and resurrection of the Lord Jesus in baptism, the Eucharist, and the other sacraments is not an isolated reality. It echoes the fundamental pattern by which we live. We give our lives in service for the sake of others, and we bring those acts of service to the altar in the Eucharist as the sacrifice of our lives to God the Father. When we do so, we join our lives to the eternal sacrifice of Jesus. In the Eucharist we find the deepest interpretation of our lives. It provides our fundamental sense of the world.

The Eucharist invites us to bring to the altar all those moments in our lives where we have given life to others through service in the kingdom of God. These acts need not be dramatic, major events. They may be the simple everyday actions of our lives. But they can be patterned after the death and resurrection of the Lord. In the simplest actions of our life we know that the secret of the kingdom of God revealed by Mark is true. We find life by giving our lives in service so that others may have life. For instance, parenting involves a lifetime of sacrifice. Parents quite literally pour out their life energy for the sake of their children. But most parents will tell you that they also find life and joy in doing so. Marriage involves sacrifice for the sake of the partner. But most married people know deep in their hearts that the giving of life and love to their spouses brings happiness and fullness of life. The same thing could be said of friendship. It is in the simplest and most common experiences and relationships in our lives that we know the gospel message is true: if you give your life for the sake of others and for the sake of Jesus and the kingdom of God, you will find life in its fullness, "full measure, pressed down, shaken together, and running over" (Lk 6:38, Jerusalem Bible).

But Mark does not want us to keep this pattern at the level of our private lives and relationships alone. Mark does not think that Jesus was crucified merely for preaching love. He believes that the patterns of the world itself must be reshaped in light of this central mystery. In this section Mark teaches that service must reshape how we think about our work and the structures of our economic system. The values of the kingdom of God should change the way we think about power and how we use it in our institutions. Human relationships in government, religious institutions, education, and the law will look different if patterned after the kingdom of God. Mark wants us to rethink what it means to be a teacher, a lawyer, a salesperson, a nurse in light of the kingdom's call to serve and give life to others.

At the heart of it all lies the secret of the kingdom of God that Mark has gradually been revealing to his readers: it is by giving life to others that we find life. Those moments of sacrifice and love of others are the fullest. They are not always the easiest or most joyful moments in our lives, but they are the most meaningful. They carry a foretaste of the eternal. Something of how sacrificial service gives life became clear on September 11, 2001, when so many people in New York City, at the Pentagon, and in the skies over Pennsylvania sacrificed for the sake of others. Those were moments and hours filled with evil and terror, but they were also moments and hours of heroism and sacrifice even on behalf of strangers. They were moments that will forever define those who were involved. They may also give the American people a deeper sense of the purpose of their lives.

Deep within we know that the secret of the kingdom at the heart of Mark's gospel is true. Yet we find it hard to see and hear at times. It is difficult to hear what Mark is telling us when children throw tantrums and parenting seems to be one long uphill struggle. It is hard to believe after living through the 1990s when greed and self-centeredness were raised to the status of virtues. It is hard to see in a world in which the few consume the vast majority of the world's resources while many lack the bare necessities of life. It is hard to break the patterns of an old self and an old world and risk the conversion to a life built on the promises of God and the patterns of the story of Jesus. The seeds look small and the harvest quite distant. But if we plant the seeds, God has promised us a harvest. And if, like the woman with the hemorrhage in chapter five of Mark's gospel, we but reach out and risk breaking the old rules by simply reaching for the cloak of Jesus, there will be healing for us and for our world. At its heart the gospel of Mark is eucharistic.

Key Points for Preaching

If Mark's gospel is eucharistic, this section of the gospel invites the homilist to contemplate the Eucharist again from new angles. Just as Mark ties the Eucharist closely to the notion of service, so must the homily. The homilist can invite the congregation to bring to the altar those moments in their lives that were sacrifices for the sake of others. He or she can give them the chance to see their parenting, their marriages, and their jobs in a new light. These experiences can be seen as the stuff of the Eucharist. The Council of Trent declared dogmatically that the Mass is a real sacrifice. It is the one eternal sacrifice of Jesus. But we must not relegate this sacrifice only to the cross or the altar. This section of Mark's gospel will not allow us to isolate the central act of Jesus' life from the rest of his life or from the rest of ours. The preacher must tie the cross closely to the rest of the ministry of Jesus. Throughout that ministry Jesus lived the basic pattern of the cross in the way he gave his life for others. Living out that pattern is how the kingdom of God breaks in to human life. The preacher must also tie the cross of Jesus and the Eucharist closely to the lives of God's people and help them to see the pattern of the cross in the fabric of their everyday lives. A good homily interprets the lives of people according to the pattern of the cross and the service that reflects that sacrifice.

The homilist can also use the stories of this section of the gospel to compare the wisdom of our contemporary world with the wisdom of the kingdom of God. The wisdom of the kingdom is built on a paradox: life at its fullest and most meaningful is life given for others. Our contemporary world often embraces the opposite as wisdom. But the opposite serves only as a path to the isolation of the individual and to death. A creative homily can point out those experiences in our lives where the truth of the gospel's wisdom stands out. We need not look much further than our marriages, our friendships, and our parenting.

The theme of "the Way" is also a fruitful topic for exploration in a homily. Mark insists that it is very hard to grasp the mystery of the gospel in spite of its simplicity. The preacher might explore how taking one small step in the direction of service takes us just a bit deeper into the mystery of the cross. We cannot grasp the cross all at once. As he did with Peter, the Lord heals our blindness gradually. We move ever more deeply into the mystery of the kingdom with each step we take. The journey will take a lifetime, for the mystery runs deep and resistance is strong. But then what we create in that journey, fashioned in the light of the cross, will live for all eternity. Each step, each planting of a small seed, takes us a little further into the mystery.

CHAPTER NINE

CONFRONTATIONS IN JERUSALEM

Mark 11:1–12:40

What to me is the multitude of your sacrifices? says the Lord;
I have had enough of burnt offerings of rams and the fat of fed beasts;
I do not delight in the blood of bulls, or of lambs, or of goats.
When you come to appear before me,
    who asked this from your hand?
Trample my courts no more;
bringing offerings is futile; incense is an abomination to me.
New moon and sabbath and calling of convocation—
I cannot endure solemn assemblies with iniquity.
Your new moons and your appointed festivals my soul hates;
they have become a burden to me,
I am weary of bearing them.
When you stretch out your hands, I will hide my eyes from you;
even though you make many prayers, I will not listen;
your hands are full of blood.
Wash yourselves; make yourselves clean;
remove the evil of your doings from before my eyes;

cease to do evil,
learn to do good;
seek justice,
rescue the oppressed,
defend the orphan,
plead for the widow.

Isaiah 1:11–17 (NRSV)

The World of the Text

Jesus was not executed merely for preaching love and peace. Any regime centered in its own power can easily twist a gospel of peace and love to its own ends. The Roman government and the religious leaders of the Jewish people murdered Jesus not because he preached peace and love, but because he represented a threat to the status quo that kept them in power. Jesus was caught in the whirlwind between the world of the kingdom and the world of the status quo. The confrontation of those two worlds created a storm that eventually crushed him.

In the last section of the gospel Mark brought us to the heart of the mystery of the gospel: the cross. But he has us break open that box as well, for the mystery of the gospel has depths he has yet to explore. The next box we encounter is marked by a bitter conflict that will lead to the execution of Jesus as a criminal.

In this ninth section of the gospel Mark tells the story of Jesus after his arrival in Jerusalem. He describes what occurred in Jerusalem not so much as a continuation of the Galilean ministry in which Jesus brought the promises of the kingdom to fulfillment in the lives of those who believed. Rather, Mark records the work of Jesus in Jerusalem as one of prophetic confrontation. In telling the story of this conflict, he explains how the work of Jesus that began with such promise could lead to such tragedy.

Mark organizes this ninth section of the gospel in two chiastic structures. The first shows Jesus condemning the temple of Jerusalem and the Jewish religious leaders for their failure to produce a harvest. The second is a series of controversy stories that stir up a whirlwind between the world of the kingdom and the world of the status quo. The first chiastic structure contains five elements that run A B C B' A'. The A stories center on the question of authority. The B stories deal with a fig tree. The C story relates the cleansing of the Temple. The second chiastic structure contains seven elements that run A B C D C′ B′ A′. Here the A stories condemn the Jewish religious leadership. The B elements interpret passages from the Psalms. The C elements discuss proper tribute to God. The centerpiece, the D story, discusses the question of the resurrection. This double chiastic structure gives the ninth section of the gospel the following overall structure:

First chiastic structure:

A Jesus' Messianic authority celebrated in the entrance to Jerusalem.
> B The cursing of the fig tree.
>> C The cleansing of the temple.
> B′ The fig tree is withered.
A′ Jesus authority is questioned.

Second chiastic structure:

A Parable of the vineyard: the condemnation of the Jewish leadership.
> B Interpretation of Psalm 118:22–23.
>> C The question of taxes: on tribute to God.
>>> D Will there be a resurrection?
>> C′ The great commandment: on tribute to God.
> B′ Interpretation of Psalm 110:1.
A′ The condemnation of the Jewish scribes.

The question of authority dominates the first part of this section. The first A story proclaims and celebrates the authority of Jesus as he enters the city of Jerusalem. The people shout blessings to celebrate the coming of the kingdom of David. They proclaim the arrival of the Messiah at his sacred capital city. This triumphal entry into Jerusalem at the time of the Passover would have been enough to put the Roman authorities on their guard. The Romans viewed any assertion of local authority without their approval as an early sign of revolution. They did not put up with popular movements for long. The Romans preferred to shed blood early so as to be rid of a possible threat rather than let revolutionary movements fester and grow.

The Messianic themes are clear in the entry of Jesus into Jerusalem. Mark, however, does not emphasize them. He believes Jesus is the

Messiah, but he does not think that this title takes the reader deep enough into the mystery of the kingdom. The title carries too many political overtones. Earlier in the gospel, in the eighth chapter, Peter had proclaimed Jesus as the Messiah. Mark told his readers that Jesus immediately moved to another level by changing the title to the Son of Man, a title associated more closely with the end-time and the coming of the kingdom of God. In this present section Mark also deflects attention away from the notion of Messiah with its implications of kingship and political power. Jesus does not stay in Jerusalem. He never spends a night in the city of David until he is forced to do so by his arrest on Holy Thursday. That one night that he stayed in Jerusalem would be the last of his earthly life. Mark also depicts Jesus going to the Temple area after his dramatic entry into the city and, after looking all around, leaving the city. Mark comments that the hour was already late. Time was running out. Not only was the death of Jesus approaching, but the end of time as well.

Why this lack of interest in messianic themes? Mark answers clearly as the first chiastic structure moves toward its center. He uses the B elements, which feature the fig tree, as a parable that explains his hesitation. The first B story in 11:12–14 shows Jesus and the Twelve on their way back into the city the next morning. Jesus, who was hungry, went over to a fig tree looking for something to eat. Finding nothing, he curses the fig tree so that no one will ever eat of its fruit again. Mark notes that it was not even the season for the poor tree to be producing fruit. The second B story in 11:20–25 takes place the next morning. On their way into the city again the disciples and Jesus find the fig tree withered to its roots. Peter comments on the fact, and Jesus replies by saying that if his disciples have faith, they can move mountains. Therefore his disciples should be steadfast in prayer, trusting that what they ask is already theirs. In prayer they are to forgive whatever has been done to them so that the Father may forgive them as well.

This dialogue begins to make some sense if we remember to keep our eye on the central proclamation of the gospel: the kingdom of God is at hand. The kingdom is to be at the center of our prayer and our lives. We are to pray and live as if it is already given, including forgiveness and the healing of human relationships. But why would anyone pray to have this poor fig tree wither?

The C story in 11:15–19 provides the central clue. Jesus goes into the Temple and drives out those who are selling, buying, and changing money. The Temple, which was meant to be a house of prayer, has become a place of business. Further, the Temple was meant to serve all peoples as a place of prayer. Mark's theme of the inclusion of the Gentiles echoes again in this story. The cleansing of the Temple was not a sudden tirade on the part of Jesus. In 11:11 Mark states that right after his triumphant entry into the city Jesus went to the Temple and observed everything that was going on there. Jesus responds to what he saw the next day. His action is symbolic like that of many of the prophets. Just as Jeremiah walked around Jerusalem wearing a yoke warning the people of Jerusalem that they would wear the yoke of submission to the Babylonians (Jer 27), so Jesus' cleansing of the Temple prophetically proclaims that the Temple has ceased to bear fruit. Like the fig tree, it has been cursed and will wither.

Mark probably wrote his gospel sometime between 65 and 70 A.D. By then, the Jews of Palestine had revolted against the Roman Empire. A large army had Jerusalem surrounded and would soon destroy the city and its Temple. Mark tells his readers why. The Temple and its city no longer served their purpose. They no longer bore fruit. They had to give way to something greater, the coming of the kingdom of God. Thus, after the Twelve have marveled at the fact that the fig tree has withered, Jesus tells them to pray and great things will happen. God will do away with whatever stands in the way of the coming of the kingdom. God will lift up any obstacle and cast it into the sea, back into the primal chaos.

Jesus is clearly repudiating the religious authority of his day. As a layman he has challenged the authority of the priests and scribes who were in charge of the Temple, and he has set aside the religious tradition that held Jerusalem and the Temple as sacred. In the second A story the leaders quickly challenge Jesus and ask him on what authority he is doing these things. Any answer is bound to fail in their eyes, for their authority derives from the Temple and the Jewish religion, an authority founded by God. Jesus avoids their trap by refusing to answer their question until they tell him by what authority John baptized. The leaders refuse to answer. If they say that John baptized of his own accord, they will be in trouble with the people, who believed John's authority came from

God. If they say it came from God, they face a double problem. They must then give some reason for their lack of belief in John, and they must admit that there is an authority at work in the land over which they have no control. The latter problem holds the key. For not only did John act with authority, but so did Jesus. That new authority has moved beyond the religious world over which they hold sway. Something new has broken into the world.

The A stories of the second chiastic structure condemn the authority of the leaders of this old world. The first of these A stories is the parable of the vineyard in 12:1-9. The owner is unable to get any fruit from the vineyard that he has so carefully planted. Those whom he leaves to care for it mistreat his representatives and kill his son. The vineyard has produced a harvest, but the Lord of the vineyard receives nothing from those he left to care for it. The parable ends quite suddenly with the statement that the owner will destroy the tenants and give the vineyard to others. The authorities in Jerusalem know exactly at whom Jesus aims this parable. He is condemning them for their failure to deliver the harvest.

In the second A story in 12:38-40 Jesus again condemns the Jewish leadership. This time he challenges the scribes because they love to make a show of their religion and their authority, but they do not keep the deeper meaning of the Law. They appropriate the property of widows, the poorest of the poor. Jesus simply states that their sentence will be more severe. The new order of the kingdom of God will see justice restored for those whom the present order has left impoverished.

The first B element in 12:10-12 adds fuel to the fire. Jesus uses Psalm 118:22-23 to further the point of the parable of the vineyard. The stone rejected by the builders has become the cornerstone. What the old world thought was crazy or evil in the second and third sections of Mark's gospel becomes the cornerstone of the new world of the kingdom which God is establishing. The old world must give way as the new world appears on the horizon. The Jewish leaders understand the message clearly and want to arrest Jesus, but they do not do so because they are afraid of the crowds.

Like the first B story, the second in 12:35-37 interprets a passage from the Psalms. This story goes to the heart of several themes in this section. Jesus cites Psalm 110:1:

The Lord said to my Lord: Sit at my right hand
And I will put your enemies under your feet. (Jerusalem Bible)

Jesus points out that the Christ is the Son of David, a Messianic title. Why then, he asks, does David, the presumed author of the psalms, call him Lord in this passage? Mark means to show that the ministry of Jesus involves something greater than what is implied in the title Messiah, and provides a scriptural basis for this view. Further, something new and unknown is at work in the gospel of Mark. Jesus' authority is that of the new age, the kingdom of God. This authority, which the Jewish leadership cannot recognize, transcends anything that has gone before

The C elements in the second chiastic structure of this ninth section of the gospel deal with paying proper tribute to God. The first story is the question about taxes in 12:13–17. The Pharisees and Herodians want to undermine Jesus' authority and so set a trap for him. They ask him if the Jewish people should pay Roman taxes. Any answer is bound to get Jesus in trouble. If he says no, the Romans will be able to bring another charge against him. If he says yes, Jesus alienates all those who resent Roman rule by approving the taxes of the hated empire. Jesus neatly eludes the trap. He asks to see a Roman coin used for payment of the tax; the coin bears the image of Caesar. Jesus tells his adversaries to give Caesar what belongs to Caesar, but to give God what belongs to God.

Jesus' answer is not an early doctrine of the separation of church and state. He does not tell us what belongs to Caesar and what belongs to God. The fact that he uses a Roman coin bearing the image of Caesar clearly implies that he had no problem with paying Roman taxes. Mark does not picture Jesus in any way siding with the revolutionaries of Jesus' world who would go to war with Rome in 65 A.D.

But what is it that belongs to God? Mark answers in the second C story found in 12:28–34. Quite simply everything belongs to God and should be given to God. A scribe asks Jesus what the greatest of all the commandments is. Jesus replies that it is to love God with all our hearts, with all our souls, with all our minds, and with all our strength. And he adds we are to love our neighbors as we love ourselves. All of the law is based on these two commandments. We simply owe God everything. We are to give our whole lives to God and live entirely for the sake of God. The kingdom asks us to take the seeds of our lives and plant them in the service of others and of God. Jesus has promised that a great harvest will follow. The kingdom will come when the disciples of Jesus have enough faith in those promises to give their whole lives to the future that God has promised. With God at the center, all things are possible. The old order will give way, and the kingdom will come. Without God at the center, destruction looms. In Mark's time the Roman armies already surrounded Jerusalem and the Temple, which had failed to produce fruit.

The central story of the second chiastic structure presents the argument with the Sadducees over the resurrection in 12:18–27. As the focal story, it contains the central teaching of the section. The Sadducees were conservatives. They did not accept the notion of the resurrection of the just, a belief which had come late to Judaism. So they challenged Jesus with the paradox of a woman who married seven different brothers, each one taking her as wife after his older brother had died. If there is resurrection, they ask, how can she have seven husbands after they rise from the dead? Does this not make the notion of resurrection a bit absurd? Jesus answers that there is no marriage in heaven. That answer takes care of the Sadducees' paradox. But then Jesus pushes the argument further by asking how God can be the God of the living if God is the God of Abraham, Isaac and Jacob, who have died. God is the God of the living, and thus these patriarchs must be alive in God.

The key phrase in the story comes when Jesus says, "God is God, not of the dead, but of the living." The gospel will not end in death but in resurrection. In the midst of all this controversy in Jerusalem the central word is a word of life. The cross dominates the horizon of Mark's gospel. Jesus cannot avoid it after the prophetic confrontations he has had with the authorities in this section. Death will now have its say, and it looks as if death's word will be final. But the gospel proclaims that the kingdom will bring life to those who give their lives totally to God. Jesus has lived in the light of God's promises of the kingdom. The God of the living has yet to speak his final and ultimate word in response to the cross.

Reflections in Front of the Text

In the theology of Paul Tillich, idolatry is at the heart of sin. False worlds are built on idols. In the confrontations that take place in Jerusalem Jesus faces such a false world.

Sin begins with what Tillich calls unbelief, a turning away of the human spirit from God as its center. When we no longer love God with our whole heart, our whole soul, our whole mind, and all our strength, hubris follows. We elevate ourselves to a status beyond the limited creatures that we are and make ourselves the center of our worlds. This situation cannot last, however. Human beings are questioners and seekers with an infinite longing at the center of our spirits. We cannot be the answer to the deepest questions that we have. And so we begin to look to creatures for the answers to our infinite longings. We turn to power, sexuality, wealth, fame, the next technological gadget, or the control that knowledge gives to find meaning in our lives. We build worlds on the foundation of some created reality that has become the center of our lives. It becomes our god. We may not worship it with religious rituals, but we serve it with our time, our energy, and our lives. We love it with all our hearts. Such is the false world of idolatry.

Perhaps the most common form of this idolatry in the late twentieth and early twenty-first century can be seen in the way a person's career can take over his or her life. Slowly it consumes all the energy and the time a person has to give. Little is left over for family or friends. Little is left even for the things a person hoped to buy with all the earnings from the career. The career becomes one's life.

The problem, however, is that such idols cannot truly give us life. They cannot, for example, conquer the physical and spiritual reality of death, nor can they provide the depth of spirit, the meaning, and the love we long for. They are not able to sustain the human spirit with its deep capacity for wisdom and truth, for beauty and love, and for justice and life. But as idolaters we do not know where else to turn, for we have turned our backs on God, who alone is the source and fulfillment of all that we desire. Limited creatures may possess us, but they do not communicate to us the power and the status of the God we long for. Originally created in goodness, they become the instruments of physical and spiritual death. They become sources of evil, not in themselves, but in the distorted roles they play as foundations of the false worlds we have built on them. When our false worlds are challenged, we rise up to defend these idols. We define ourselves in terms of them, and we use other human beings as a means to gain them.

Tillich also points out that religion itself can become such an idol. Its Scriptures, dogmas, and various practices can become ends in themselves, a means to control God. In the dynamics of such a distorted religious life, the self remains at the center, and God becomes a tool to serve our happiness. The distortions caused by such false religions are even worse than secular idols, for religion speaks in the name of the ultimate. But what such religion raises to ultimate status is the authority of religious leaders and systems of government in religion, or particular ways of articulating religious truth, or particular religious practices. These are sacred because they point to God, but they are not God. They can become tools in our own power games so that those in power see anyone who challenges them or questions them as evil. Acting in the name of the ultimate, the proponents of such false religion assume the right to crush those who disagree. They act in the name of God, but they no longer represent God in their actions. In these ways religion becomes idolatry.

Jesus embodies true religion, and in his actions and words he confronted the false worlds and false religions of his day. This section of Mark's gospel not only tells the story of that confrontation but also points out to the reader the qualities of true religion.

True religion recognizes that God is the God of the living, not of the dead. God alone can give life—not just physical life, but life in its fullness with the meaning, the depth, and the purpose we desire. To live for anything but the mystery of the God of life, whom we can in no way control, limit, or reduce to some finite thing is to embrace death. One must love God alone with one's whole heart, one's whole soul, one's whole mind, and all one's strength.

This section of the gospel draws an inseparable connection between the two great commandments. The love of God and the love of our neighbor lie at the heart of true religion. The previous section of the gospel illustrated what that love of neighbor means: we must serve one another with the very stuff of our lives. The mystery of the kingdom in

Mark's gospel is quite simple. We discover the kingdom in our midst when we use our lives to bestow the gifts of the kingdom on others. True religion and its authority bring about the kingdom of God for others.

This section of the gospel reveals a new authority in Jesus, an authority that goes beyond anything the Jewish tradition had previously known. Jesus is more than a prophet; he is more than the messiah. He is the one who brings the kingdom of God. He does so not only in his teaching, but also through his ministry which is centered on bringing the promises of God to fulfillment for others. Eventually he will pour out his lifeblood for the sake of the life of the world. Institutional boundaries cannot contain such religion or its authority.

The truth of Jesus' life is not limited to those who came to know his name and chose to be his disciples. It could be found among many faithful Jews of his time. Those who never heard his name but loved God with their whole hearts and gave their lives for others knew the true religion which Jesus taught his followers. Jesus brings to full expression and full actualization what God has been working out in human hearts since the beginning of time.

Such a life challenges all false worlds and all false religions. For Jesus' life shows forth clearly the lie of a life, or a world, or a religion centered solely on the self. That false world, represented politically by the Romans and religiously by the Jewish leadership, struck out at Jesus to defend its legitimacy and its power. The whirlwind and chaos that emerge in the human spirit when worlds are challenged crushed him. But death would not have the last word, for the God of Jesus is the God of the living, not of the dead.

In that sense Jesus was indeed killed for preaching love.

Key Points for Preaching

This section of the gospel revolves around two themes: authority and resurrection. We must understand these themes in the light of what it means to pay proper tribute to God.

It is hard to preach on battles over authority that took place centuries ago. But the same issues about the use of authority haunt us in our own time. Authority and power do not exist for their own sake. They exist for the sake of bringing life to others. Authority is integral to the lives of the congregation who hear our homilies and sermons. A good homilist cannot avoid the topic, for God's people deal with authority in politics and religion, in their economics, educational institutions, and families. Far too often authority becomes an instrument for our own ends and can reduce others to mere instruments. Mark's gospel states clearly that we are to use authority for the sake of others. Authentic power gives life to others.

A second powerful theme in this section is the notion that God is a God of life. The homilist can preach this theme by itself and explore how God wills the full life of his people. God has set his heart on life for his people in their jobs, their families, their friendships and loves. God desires that they find the meaning, joy, and depth that are the fullness of life. The preacher can also combine the theme of life with that of power. Ultimate power is in the hands of God. God created all that exists and holds the cosmos in being. God always uses power in creation and in history for the sake of others. The story of Jesus reveals that most clearly. The life of Jesus is the fullness of the revelation of God, who is life and love.

Finally, this section of the gospel emphasizes proper tribute to God. The homilist can emphasize that the proper tribute to God is to live as images of God. We image God by loving as God loves, by using our power and our lives to bring the fullness of life to others. In doing so we not only image God in history. We come to share the very life of God which Jesus has made known.

CHAPTER TEN

THE DISCOURSE ON THE END OF TIME

Mark 12:41–13:37

Who will see that all past time is driven back by the future,
that the future is consequent on the past,
and all past and future are created and take their course
from that which is ever present.

St. Augustine, *The Confessions*, Book 11, chapter 11

Then must thou needs find out new heaven and new earth.

William Shakespeare, *Anthony and Cleopatra*, I, i, 17

The World of the Text

In the previous section Mark recounted how Jesus' days in Jerusalem were filled with conflict that would lead to his arrest and execution. Now that we have broken open that box, Mark has us look even more deeply at the mystery of the kingdom. Earlier he noted that after Jesus first arrived in Jerusalem, he looked around the Temple complex and immediately left the city because it was late. This new box of the mystery contemplates how late the hour truly is.

As we saw in the first section of the gospel, Mark writes against the background of apocalyptic expectations. The fullness of time has arrived; the kingdom of God is at hand. We must orient everything in our lives to the nearness of God's promises. Early in the gospel, however, Mark downplayed the cosmic symbols usually associated with apocalyptic expectations: the earth shaking to its foundations; the heavenly light of the sun, the moon, and the stars going out; the armies of good and evil waging one great final battle; and God re-creating a new heaven and a new earth. Instead, Mark emphasized God's re-creating the landscape of the human spirit by healing bodies and spirits, by casting evil out of the lives of people, and by opening a hope-filled future to people.

In this next section of the gospel, Mark 12:41—13:37, Mark unleashes the full power of apocalyptic symbolism. Only once before in Mark have we heard an extended teaching of Jesus. Like that first sermon in the fourth chapter, the discourse in this section commands our attention because Mark has told us over and over that Jesus was teaching, but he has not told us what Jesus said. Now we get to hear Jesus teach again. But, just as that first discourse of Jesus gave us difficult parables of seeds and mysterious sayings about hidden lamps, this second extended sermon of Jesus in the thirteenth chapter of the gospel contains material just as difficult to understand.

Mark sets up this sermon with three introductory statements. The first relates the story of the widow at the end of chapter twelve. She places everything she has at God's service by putting it all in the temple treasury. She stands in stark contrast to Jesus' opponents, the leaders of the Jewish people and the temple officials, whom in the previous passage Jesus had condemned for "swallowing" the property of widows. More important, though, is the symbolic role this widow plays. She gives everything, little though it is. Her actions echo the parable of the mustard seed, which though small becomes great, and the multiplication of the loaves and fish, in which a little food feeds a great multitude. Her actions also reflect Jesus' teaching after the first passion prediction that we must give our entire lives in order to find life in its fullness and Jesus' later statement that we must love God with our whole hearts, souls, and lives. Her trust allows the kingdom to burst forth in its fullness.

In the second introductory statement Jesus responds to the awe his disciples show at the magnificence of the temple and its buildings. He simply states that the entire complex will be destroyed. Not one stone will be left on another. As the last section emphasized, the old world is no longer bearing fruit, and it must give way to the new world God is creating. The movements of Jesus in the early part of this section of the gospel reinforce this statement. He begins in 12:41 sitting opposite the temple, where the disciples make their comment about its glory and to which Jesus responds. In 13:3 he has moved to the Mount of Olives facing the temple. These movements recall those of the glory of God in Ezekiel 10:18—11:25, when the divine presence left the temple, paused on the hills east of Jerusalem for moment, and then abandoned Jerusalem and the temple for good. The destruction of the city by the Babylonians followed.

The disciples make the final introductory statement when they ask Jesus in 13:4, "when will this happen, and what sign will there be when all these things are about to come to an end?" (NAB). Ambiguity pervades this question. "All these things" might refer to the destruction of Jerusalem, or it might refer to the end of time and the coming of the kingdom. Given the nature of the discourse that follows and the major themes of the gospel, Mark most likely wants this ambiguity. He wants Jesus to speak about the imminent destruction of the city and about the ultimate coming of the kingdom at the end of time.

Mark uses this second discourse of Jesus to address a number of crucial issues in his first-century community. As we saw before, Mark wrote about the time of the first Jewish revolt against the Roman Empire, which took place from 65 to 70 A.D. His readers must have wondered about the import of this war and whether they ought to fight to save the sacred city of Jerusalem, the city of the Messiah. Was this the apocalyptic war of the end-time in which God would defeat the forces of evil and oppression and set up God's kingdom in place of the empire? Jesus answers with an unequivocal no. The war with the Romans is not the apocalyptic battle. His disciples are to get out of town; they are to flee to the mountains. This is not their war. In the previous section Mark has made clear the judgment of God and Jesus on the sacred city and the temple. They no longer produce fruit, and so they are to be destroyed. Mark's attitude toward the sacred city and its temple theology finds its roots in their spiritual failure and in his judgment that Christians are not called upon to fight this war.

Mark's aversion to this war also explains his guardedness in the use of the title of Messiah for Jesus. He does not reject it, for he calls Jesus the Messiah in the opening verse of the gospel. But he does not use it a great deal in the narrative of the gospel. When Peter uses the title in 8:29 and the high priest does likewise in 14:61, Jesus immediately substitutes the title of the apocalyptic Son of Man. Messiah bore too many political overtones. Probably Jewish leaders in the war claimed this title for themselves and asked people to rally to their messianic leadership to defend Jerusalem. Jesus warns in 13:22: "False messiahs and false prophets will appear and produce signs and omens, to lead astray, if possible, the elect" (NRSV). Mark wants his community to be clear about how they are to respond to this crisis. The true Messiah has no part in this war.

If the Jewish revolt of 65-70 A.D. is not the war of the end-time and yet the end-time draws near, where exactly are we in time? When will everything be fulfilled? This question was likely uppermost in the minds of Mark's community. Jesus answers that there will be wars and rumors of wars. False Messiahs will come in the name of Jesus and claim to be Jesus. There will be great struggles among nations. All this augurs the birth pangs of the kingdom. But the true end of time and coming of the kingdom still lies in the future (13:5–8). When will the kingdom come in its fullness? The Son and the angels do not know, only the Father (13:32–33). But we do know there is time yet before the end. In Mark's sense of time we live at the approach of the end, but a bit of time yet remains before the Lord's return with the fullness of God's promises.

What are we to do with this time? We must spread the news of the gospel and bring the reality of the kingdom into the lives of as many people as possible. Mark's sense of the shortness of the time remaining explains the urgency in his gospel. It is the reason Mark is so strict in his norms for discipleship in chapter ten. He insists that we cannot let money, or relationships, or any other finite concern keep us from giving ourselves totally to the reality of the kingdom of God. Jesus warns in 13:9–13 that proclaiming the kingdom and challenging the world will bring persecution to the disciples. Just as John the Baptist and Jesus were handed over, Mark uses the same Greek verb to predict that the disciples too will be handed over and suffer for the sake of the kingdom. But the end will come.

> But in those days, after that suffering, the sun will be darkened, and the moon will not give its light, and the stars will be falling from heaven, and the powers in the heavens will be shaken. Then they will see "the Son of Man coming in clouds" with great power and glory. Then he will send out the angels, and gather his elect from the four winds, from the ends of the earth to the ends of heaven. From the fig tree learn its lesson: as soon as its branch becomes tender and puts forth its leaves, you know that summer is near. So also, when you see these things taking place, you know that he is near, at the very gates. Truly I tell you, this generation will not pass away until all these things have taken place. Heaven and earth will pass away, but my words will not pass away (13:24–27, NRSV).

The Greek word βλεπω (to look, to see) echoes throughout this discourse. It is the first word that Jesus uses in the discourse, and he repeats it as a command in 13:5, 9, 23, and 33. The last word of the discourse bears a similar command to watch. The issue of seeing and perceiving correctly, which has been so prominent in the gospel, is now even more urgent. In the midst of the struggles that discipleship suffers in the chaotic storm between worlds, we must keep our eyes on the kingdom.

Reflections in Front of the Text

It is a terrible thing to be lost in time.

As he meditates on the nature of time in the eleventh book of his *Confessions*, Augustine notes that all we have is the present. The past is gone and the future has yet to arrive. The only time that exists is the present. But the present also eludes us. Augustine begins with the present year, but then notes that some of its months have slipped into the past and some still lie in the future. He finds the same to be true of a month, a day, and an hour until finally all we are left with is a tiny fraction of a moment. Scientists who deal in nanoseconds could strip the present moment down to an infinitesimal fraction. Humans are temporal beings. We live in time, but our anchor in time is slippery.

Mircea Eliade, a historian of religion, mentions of the terror of history in his work, *The Myth of the Eternal Return*. The radical emphasis on human autonomy in the modern world has cut the ties of the present from participation in anything that transcends the moment and brings it meaning and direction. Archaic peoples, Eliade argues, overcame the fear of empty time with their cyclical sense of reality. Time begins again with each year, and human life finds enduring value by repeating the eternal patterns of the gods. But for those who live in linear time, time that moves from an unrepeatable beginning to an indefinite end, life in time becomes a struggle to create meaning in one unique moment after another. The burden can be daunting.

Paul Tillich states that time swallows all its creations. Things precious in the present moment are lost all too soon to the past. Despite the billions of dollars we spend each year on film for cameras and other recording devices, we cannot hold on to the present. Under the power of sin, cut off from the eternal, time becomes mere transitoriness. The temptation, Tillich says, is to avoid the emptiness by filling the present with idols. History is full of false messiahs who lead crusades to save the towers of Babel they have built.

But time is not empty. The creation accounts of Genesis tell us that God created with a purpose and that human beings are central to that purpose. Paul Tillich speaks of the "Eternal Now," those moments in our lives where something more is present. Something of the divine fills those sacred moments and gives our lives direction and meaning. A spiritual presence lives on in us, a foretaste of the beauty, the justice, the truth, the love, and the union that comes to its fullness only in God. It is only a foretaste, but it feeds our spirits and guides our lives. We have tasted the kingdom of God, and our lives take on purpose as we long for its fullness.

Mark's gospel is full of such foretastes. Every healing, every time evil is driven out of a human life, every word of forgiveness, every life made whole is pregnant with the possibilities of life in its fullness. Disciples abandon their boats and livelihoods to follow Jesus; widows give their last pennies; Simon of Cyrene is ready to take up the cross.

Mark lets his reader know that time is far from empty. The whole gospel proclaims that the fullness of time is here; the kingdom of God is at hand. But in this section Mark also warns us to be watchful. We have a tendency to fill the void with temporal concerns. We are tempted to make these concerns ultimate and give them our whole hearts, lives, and energy. But they eventually fade into the past. Thus Mark warns us against the calls of false messiahs and against crusades to save what cannot last.

What will last? Mark has told us story after story of things that last: bread shared with others; a cup of water given to the least; a word of forgiveness; the healing embrace of someone who is struggling. Anything marked by a love of God at its center and by service to others shares in some mysterious way in the eternal life of God. It fills our time with meaning and gives our lives direction. It is worth giving our lives for.

Mark does not believe that we are lost in meaningless time. He knows exactly where we are. The end is near and the fullness of the kingdom hovers on the horizon. Jesus will return soon. The period of history in which Mark's Christian community is situated has lasted much longer than Mark anticipated; yet Mark's message is pertinent to us today. We still have time, but the kingdom is on the horizon. What are we to do with that time? Mark repeats the word "look" or "watch" several times in this section. We are to watch for the signs of the kingdom in our own time, and then give our last two cents to bring it about for others. Then the kingdom will dawn in its fullness for all.

Key Points for Preaching

Preaching on the eschatological discourse is difficult. No one believes we are anywhere near the end of history. Even the passing of the last millennium served more as a time for partying than a time to prepare for the coming of the judgment day. Our chief worry was whether our computers would work the next day.

But we are temporal beings. We do not simply have time, like any other commodity; we are temporal at the core of our very being. This deserves the attention of the homilist every now and then. A good preacher must locate people in time. A homily can call people back from that thin edge of the slippery present that Augustine describes. It can help us recognize that we sometimes desperately try to hang on to the past with video cameras and recording devices. God's people need to be reminded that we live in a present pregnant with meaning and with the presence of the power of God. The present can give birth to the new possibilities of the kingdom of God.

The preacher can help us recall the moments of our own lives in which we experienced the presence of the Eternal Now: the first time we held our child; a moment when we know we are loved; the peace that comes with forgiveness; the look of hope in someone who has just taken up a challenge. The preacher can call us to trust these moments as seeds of the future. Through a good sermon the homilist can help us to plant those seeds, sharing the richness God has bestowed on us with others so that their fullness might grow and the presence of the kingdom might mature into a great harvest. The preacher can help the congregation to watch alertly for the coming of the fullness of time suspended on the horizon of each of our lives.

CHAPTER ELEVEN

THE HEART OF THE MYSTERY: THE PASSION NARRATIVE

Mark 14:1–15:47

Let us proclaim the Mystery of Faith:
Christ has died,
Christ is risen,
Christ will come again.

The Eucharistic Prayer of the Roman liturgy

Mark now brings his readers to the heart of the mystery of the gospel, the mystery of the death and resurrection of Jesus. It is highly likely that the passion narrative was already circulating among the early Christian communities before Mark retells it here in his own words. But in Mark's version it echoes with the themes he has developed throughout his gospel. This is not surprising, for all that Mark has written so far is intended to prepare the reader to grasp the central mystery of Christianity. He expressed this mystery in parables and sayings in the fourth section of the gospel. He showed it again in symbolic form in the two miracles of the loaves in the seventh section. Finally he stated it clearly in the eighth section in the three passion predictions and his reflections on the nature of discipleship.

Every act of Jesus' ministry has been a proclamation of the paschal mystery, for Jesus is always opening the possibilities of life to people in his miracles, his exorcisms and forgiveness, and his teaching. Through his ministry a taste of the fullness of life that is resurrection in the kingdom of God becomes a reality for those with faith. Now in the eleventh and twelfth sections Mark reveals the mystery, clearly embodied in the death of Jesus and his resurrection. By giving his life totally for others in faithfulness to the Father's promises, Jesus opens to all creation the fullness of life in the resurrection.

Mark has provided other hints as well to prepare the reader for the cross. In the very first chapter just before the proclamation of the gospel in 1:15, Mark tells us that John the Baptist had been handed over. In section six we see exactly what being handed over implies: John is executed. The opposition against Jesus was already developing in the second section, and by the end of that section in 3:6 the authorities are already plotting against Jesus. Opposition continues to develop when Mark compares the responses to Jesus in sections three and six. Finally, the chaos that threatens to engulf people as they look into the abyss that lies between the world they have known and the world of the kingdom prompts some to react with violence to protect the status quo.

Mark not only brings the mystery of the gospel to its full expression in the Passion narrative; he also continues to explore other themes of his gospel. He continues to use one-dimensional characters to compare the responses of people to the crisis of two worlds colliding. He develops further the struggle of discipleship by concentrating on the response of the Twelve, especially Peter. And he no longer shies away from the title Messiah, but reworks its meaning and embraces it because the context is right for doing so.

Mark opens the passion narrative with a chiastic structure that again compares the responses of some undeveloped figures to those of Jesus. The structure has three elements so that it runs A B A' in 14:1–11. The A elements move the story forward by telling first of the plotting of the chief priests and scribes to put Jesus to death and then of Judas' betrayal. These hostile responses surround the anointing of Jesus by an unknown woman during a dinner party in Bethany. This woman's action is one of great courage and compassion and stands in stark contrast to the murderous plots and treachery of the A elements. Her act is also ambiguous. The reader could easily interpret it as the anointing of a king, the Messiah. The timing is right for such an act, for Jesus has recently entered Jerusalem, the city of the Messiah, where he is hailed as the one who has come in the name of David.

Mark, however, has Jesus interpret it as the anointing of his body for its imminent death. This interpretation does not make a great deal of sense, for bodies are prepared for burial by anointing only after the person has died. Mark is reworking something here. He has taken an act that would be appropriate for the welcoming of the Messiah to his city and turned it into the preparation for his death. In a very subtle way he is moving the notion of Messiah in the direction of the image of one who suffers and dies. He continues to recast this title in that direction throughout this section of the gospel.

Mark also moves the plot toward the death of Jesus by inserting another reminder that the disciples will not always have Jesus with them (14:7). The time of his death and resurrection is at hand. The work of the kingdom will be in the hands of his disciples. He has prepared his disciples for this moment, beginning with their first missionary journey in the sixth section of the gospel.

After the preparations for the Passover supper are made in 14:12–16, Mark has another three-part chiastic structure that compares responses to the coming of the kingdom. The A elements are Jesus' foretelling the betrayal of Judas and the denial of Peter. The B element is the Markan account of the institution of the Eucharist. The A elements give us another close look at the struggle of discipleship through the lens of the Twelve. As the cross, the heart of the mystery of the kingdom, approaches, Judas turns back to the world he had left to follow Jesus. He is ready to betray Jesus for money. Peter protests his courage, but Jesus knows it will fail. Faced with the powerful opposition of the old order, Peter will deny Jesus. The smallness of the seed of the kingdom will overwhelm him.

At the center of the chiastic structure lies the institution of the Eucharist. Jesus uses bread once again to give himself for the sake of those whom he loves. This time the miracle of bread is not one of multiplication but of transformation. Bread becomes his body and wine becomes his blood. He will give them up for the sake of many. In section six of the gospel Jesus used a few loaves of bread to feed thousands. He took what he possessed and gave it for the sake of others. Now he does the same with his very life, his very being. He will give himself for the sake of others. The Eucharistic action at this Passover meal anticipates the total giving of self on the part of Jesus: the final act that makes the fullness of the kingdom possible.

The story of Jesus at prayer in Gethsemane advances the struggle of discipleship one great step further. The twelve continue to flounder. Jesus warns them to watch using the same verb γρηγορειτε that ended the eschatological discourse of section ten and that echoes the repetition of the word βλεπω in that sermon. Later, finding them asleep, Jesus warns them again, using the same word, "watch," so that they might not be put to the test. The Greek word for "test" (πειρασμον) is the same word used in 1:13 for the great eschatological struggle between Satan and Jesus in the desert. Now Jesus tells Peter to pray that he may keep his eye on the kingdom and may not be overcome in the chaotic struggle between the world of the kingdom and the world he has left behind.

Remarkably we see Jesus himself struggling with faithfulness to the kingdom. Faced with the prospect of a horrible death the next day, he asks the Father to take away this trial. But no other way lies open to him. If Jesus stays faithful to the kingdom, he will upset the powers that be, and they will come for him. Recognizing this, he submits to the will of God and remains faithful to the promises of the kingdom of God.

In the story of Jesus' arrest in the garden (14:43–52), the Twelve reach the lowest point in their struggle to be faithful to the kingdom. All of them desert Jesus, the one who brings the kingdom. Judas descends even lower. He betrays Jesus with a kiss. He uses the sign of friendship and love to hand over the one in whom he had once placed his deepest hopes. If to live for the kingdom is to love God with your whole heart and soul, Judas has taken the token of that love and turned it to treachery for the sake of money, whose promises of happiness and life are empty.

Peter presents a different aspect of the struggle of discipleship. The trial of Jesus before the Sanhedrin sits in the middle of another three-part chiastic structure in which the figure of Peter surrounds the questioning of Jesus by the high priest and his retinue (14:53–72). Chapter

14:66–72 tells of the failure of Peter as three times he denies any relationship or knowledge of Jesus. Yet the figure of Peter in this section is ambiguous, for Mark notes that he followed Jesus (14:54). The Greek uses the verb ακολουθεω which means to follow or to be a disciple. Peter remains faithful, but he is still stumbling. As the Jewish leadership try Jesus and condemn him to death, Peter still cannot see clearly that the only way to realize the promises of the kingdom is to sacrifice himself for others as Jesus is doing in the midst of his trial.

Peter is also caught between these two conflicting worlds, as the enemies of Jesus attempt to condemn Jesus for his denunciation of the present Temple and the world of meaning that it represents. When they cannot make this charge stick, they condemn Jesus for the blasphemy the Sanhedrin finds in the following testimony:

> The high priest put a second question to him saying, "Are you the Christ, the Son of the Blessed One?" "I am," said Jesus, "and you will see the Son of man seated at the right hand of the Power and coming with the clouds of heaven." (14:61–62, New Jerusalem Bible)

The Jewish leadership condemns Jesus for identifying himself as the Son of Man, the one who brings the new world of the kingdom of God. Peter is caught in the chaos between these two worlds. Blinded by the storm, he cannot see clearly yet. He tries to follow, but he fails and denies Jesus.

As the story of Jesus' death moves relentlessly forward in chapter fifteen, Mark does four things. At one level he simply tells the story in all of its stark simplicity, as he does throughout the gospel. His terse style just keeps moving forward without a great deal of comment. That stark style continues in the passion narrative.

Secondly, once we have seen the struggles to be faithful in Jesus' prayer in the garden and in Peter's continuing to follow Jesus and yet denying him, Mark illustrates responses to Jesus and his message of the kingdom of God in character types whose deeds speak loudly, but whose personalities Mark leaves undeveloped. In 15:21 Simon of Cyrene does exactly what Jesus said discipleship demands in 8:34: "If anyone wants to be a follower of mine, let him renounce himself and take up his cross and follow me" (NJB).

In 15:40–41 the women stay with Jesus to the bitter end. Mark uses the same word, ακολουθεω (to follow, to be a disciple), to describe them as he used to describe Peter when he left his nets to follow Jesus in 1:18 and when Peter follows Jesus to the trial in 14:54. Unlike Peter and the rest of the Twelve, the women remain faithful, but Mark does not develop their characters so that we might see their struggle in following Jesus.

Joseph of Arimathea, a member of the Sanhedrin, risks breaking with the rest of the Jewish leadership by daring to bury Jesus with respect. Mark uses Joseph to show that not all of the Jewish leaders rejected Jesus. Some risk their lives for the sake of the kingdom. Mark does not utter a wholesale condemnation of the Jewish people or their leaders. Rather, he condemns the old world of meaning that many of them cannot relinquish.

On the other hand, there are those who do reject Jesus. Pilate does not know what to make of the situation. He wants to release Jesus, for he recognizes that the Jewish leadership have handed Jesus over to him out of spite. In the end, Pilate simply placates the crowds who demand that Jesus be crucified. The crowds prove fickle in Mark. They hailed Jesus as Messiah during his entry into Jerusalem, but a few days later they cry out for his execution. The Roman soldiers mock Jesus. Mark employs irony in reporting their actions, for they crown Jesus with thorns, hail him as King of the Jews, and bend their knees in homage to him. Mark wants the reader to recognize that what they do in mockery should be done in earnest, for Jesus is the Messiah, the king. Finally, there are those who mock Jesus as he hangs on the cross. They challenge him to save himself and come down from the cross. Again Mark is using irony, for the cross and its ignominy will be defeated when God raises Jesus from the dead on the third day, exactly as he had foretold.

Thirdly, Mark works very hard throughout the passion narrative to reinterpret and recast the title Messiah or Christ, which is closely associated with the title "the King of the Jews." Mark does not hesitate to use the title for Jesus, as he does in the opening words of his gospel: "The beginning of the gospel about Jesus Christ, the Son of God "(1:1). But in the narrative itself he backs away from the title in 8:29ff. When Peter declares that Jesus is the Christ, Jesus immediately substitutes the title Son of Man, a title more closely associated with the end of time and the coming of the kingdom of God. Then Jesus begins to speak of his passion and death. Mark makes a similar shift in 14:61–62. The high priest asks Jesus if he is the Messiah, the Son of the Blessed One. This time Jesus answers that he is. But again he prefers the title "Son of Man" and then speaks directly of the coming of the kingdom of God by quoting Daniel 7:13: "I am," said Jesus, "and you will see the Son of man seated at the right hand of the Power and coming with the clouds of heaven." In 13:21 Jesus warns the disciples not to believe false proclamations of the Christ. In 13:22 Mark even uses the word pseudo-Christs, for those who would stir up false hopes of the kingdom. Finally, the title Christ is used to mock Jesus in 15:32 as he hangs on the cross. Again Mark uses the title ironically, for while the crowds use it to mock Jesus, Mark knows that what they are saying is true.

Mark uses the same irony in the passion narrative around the title, "King of the Jews." He ties this title closely to that of Messiah in the mocking of the crowds in 15:32: "Let the Christ, the king of Israel, come down from the cross now, for us to see it and believe" (NJB). Pilate wants to know if Jesus is claiming to be the king of the Jews (15:2), for that would brand Jesus as a revolutionary in the eyes of the Romans. The Roman soldiers mock Jesus as the King of the Jews, a charge the Romans place over his head on the cross: "The King of the Jews." But Mark does more than use the term with irony through the passion narrative. He redefines what the titles Messiah and King of the Jews mean by tying them closely to the death of Jesus. It is precisely Jesus' giving of his life for the sake of others that makes him King of the Jews and Messiah.

This notion of kingship may not make sense in the worlds of meaning called the Roman Empire and the Jewish theocracy, but in this understanding of power lies the wisdom of the world of meaning called the kingdom of God. True power and leadership are shown through the service of people who use their lives to bring about the promises of God for others. Because Mark redefines political and religious power throughout the passion narrative, he is able to properly name Jesus as King of the Jews and Christ/Messiah.

Fourthly, Mark may narrate the death of Jesus in a terse and stark manner, but he interprets these events at several points in the story. The first interpretation occurs in the narrative of the institution of the Eucharist. There Jesus gives bread, transformed into his body, to his disciples. Then he gives them the cup of wine and says that this is the cup of his blood that will be poured out for many. Against the background of the story of the ministry and teaching of Jesus, Mark uses the Eucharistic narrative to tell us that Jesus on the cross will do exactly what he taught others to do: he will find the kingdom and life by giving himself for the sake of others.

The second place where Mark interprets the passion is in the trial before the Sanhedrin. There Jesus declares that we will see the Son of Man coming upon the clouds of heaven. As the Son of Man he will bring the kingdom which Daniel prophesied and for which human hearts have longed since the beginning of time. But Jesus can bring it only through the cross. The kingdom can come only by the complete giving of self for others, and for Jesus this means the cross. In the eighth section of the gospel Jesus made it clear that his disciples must give themselves in the way they serve one another. Their lives are to be poured out in union with Jesus to bring the kingdom for others. Only in this way will the disciples find the fullness of God's promises and life.

The third interpretation of the passion comes in the final words of Jesus in 15:34: "My God, My God, why have you deserted me?". At one level Jesus is praying the opening words of Psalm 22, a psalm which begins as a lament in the midst of suffering, but moves on to praise Yahweh for his rescue of the suffering one and God's care for the peoples of the earth. This Hebrew prayer closes by talking about the sovereignty of God over all peoples. The psalm fits exactly the moment Mark is picturing in the passion narrative. Jesus suffers now in giving his life for the sake of others, but this sacrifice will lead to the triumph of God and the coming of the kingdom of God.

But even more is happening in this final prayer of Jesus. Jürgen Moltmann in his book *The Crucified God* claims we must take these last words of Jesus exactly for what they are. Jesus feels abandoned. He wonders what has happened to the promises of the kingdom in this darkest hour. Moltmann wants us to take seriously not just the physical suffering of Jesus but also the situation in which he finds himself. He has been betrayed, denied, and abandoned, and as he faces death he must be wondering where God is for him. The seeds of the kingdom must have looked very unprepossessing indeed to Jesus on the cross. Moltmann claims that Mark is making clear how deep the giving of Jesus goes in his suffering and death. Jesus not only encounters the physical fact of death, but also joins all those who have ever felt abandoned even by God, all those who cannot see any hope in their situation. The emptying of self by Jesus is complete. All that remains is to cry out to a God he cannot see. By the giving of his life in this most desperate of human situations, Jesus enables the promises of God to touch all humankind. Jesus' ministry began with his willingness to break old taboos and to risk touching the leper in 1:41. It ends with Jesus' touching the depths of human despair. Because of his willingness to enter into the human situation with us, nothing is beyond the reach of the promises of God.

The fourth place in the passion narrative where Mark interprets the death of Jesus occurs in the words of the centurion who executed Jesus and watched him die. In 15:39 the centurion declares, "Truly this man was the Son of God!" This is the third time in the gospel Jesus has been proclaimed Son of God. The first occurred at the baptism of Jesus when the voice from heaven spoke to him saying, "You are my beloved Son; with you I am well pleased" (1:11). The voice spoke to Jesus, and Mark does not say whether anyone else heard it. The second occurrence took place at the transfiguration. The voice from the cloud said to the three disciples who had accompanied Jesus up the mountain, "This is my beloved Son. Listen to him" (9:7). Finally, in the centurion's proclamation, this title is found on the lips of a human being for the first time. It is a key title for Mark, for he includes it in the title of the gospel in 1:1. But like the titles Messiah and King of the Jews, the reader can properly understand it only in the light of the death of Jesus. In Mark's mind no one can claim that there is something divine about Jesus and his mission until they have seen him give his life completely for others. Mark wants his readers to understand that the reality of the divine is deeply identified with a love that gives itself totally.

Mark interprets the death of Jesus a fifth time in the comment that follows the death of Jesus. He states that at the moment of Jesus' death the veil of the temple was torn in two from top to bottom. What Jesus has done on the cross marks the end of the old order, the world of meaning that had shown such resistance to Jesus and the kingdom of God. The hour has come (14:41); the kingdom of God is at hand.

Reflections in Front of the Text

Christian theology must deal with two great questions when it reflects on the gospel message: who is Jesus? and how is Jesus' death and resurrection redemptive?

The second question leads theology into the realm of theories of redemption. If asked how redemption took place, most Christians would respond with a version of the atonement theory, to which St. Anselm gave classic form at the end of the eleventh century. Anselm explained that humanity's sin has offended God, whose honor can only be restored by an act of infinite value. As sinners, human beings must do something to restore God's honor; but we are unable to effectively atone for our sins because nothing we can do is of infinite value. God in his mercy sent his Son to become human and, in solidarity with humanity, to offer a sacrifice of infinite value. Because the Son is divine, his sacrifice on the cross bears infinite value. Because the Son also shares with us our human nature, his sacrifice can redeem humanity. Thus, the sacrifice of the cross, a human act with infinite value, effects humanity's atonement with God. In Anselm's mind, all this took place in a context resembling the feudal courts of his medieval world. He saw God as a liege lord and humanity as one of God's many vassals. Later medieval and Reformation theology would move his theory out of the feudal court and see it in the light of a criminal court. Sin became a great and terrible crime for which the punishment was terrible and eternal. So the Son of God took on human nature and underwent the penalty for our sins. Thus he freed the human race from sin and its punishment.

Anselm's theory of atonement has multiple problems. First, it does not connect Jesus' saving act on the cross either with what he had done in his ministry up to that point or with his resurrection. Secondly, the theory in its later forms tends to picture God as an ogre who demands a bloody sacrifice to appease his offended honor. In Anselm's treatise on the topic, the *Cur Deus Homo?*, he delicately balances the justice of God with God's mercy. Justice and order are important in Anselm's world, which was just emerging from a period of chaos and warfare. Later proponents of his theory, however, emphasize the anger of God and how hard it is to appease God.

Mark does not approach the death of Jesus in any way that resembles Anselm's theory. Rather, Mark intimately connects the cross with the ministry of Jesus. The mystery of the kingdom of God lies at the heart of both the ministry of Jesus and his death. Mark understands both as expressions of the central mystery of the gospel, that when life is given for the sake of others, the promises of the kingdom flow in abundance. Mark also ties the resurrection intimately to both the cross and the ministry. By the grace of God the resurrection flows from the act of giving of one's self so that others may have life in abundance in the kingdom of God. New life, which is typified by the resurrection, occurs in every act of the gospel in which Jesus bestows the promises of the kingdom on someone who needs a miracle in his or her life. In that sense, every story of the gospel is a story of death and resurrection.

Moreover, Mark does not picture the Father as an ogre needing to be appeased. The Father does not will the terrible and bloody death of his Son. God wills that the promises of the kingdom might be realized for God's people and that Jesus and his disciples be faithful to the call of the kingdom. Given the chaos, the blindness, and the violence that the kingdom engenders on the part of those who resist it in the name of the status quo, Jesus cannot avoid the cross if he is to remain faithful to the kingdom. His prayer centered on this reality in the Garden of Gethsemane on the night before he died. No other way lay open to him than to die for the sake of the kingdom. God is not a terrible judge in Mark's gospel. Rather, God is one who offers the fullness of the promises of God's kingdom to his people and will let nothing stand in the way of those promises.

Who, then, is this Jesus who gave his life for the entire world? Mark is slow and often reluctant to make known that piece of the mystery of the kingdom. He pictures Jesus silencing those who know who he is. For instance, when the demons recognize him, Jesus rebukes them again and again and refuses to let them make him known (1:25,34; 3:12). He also tells those whom he has cured not to let anyone know about it (1:44; 5:43; 7:36; 8:26). As the disciples are given clues to his identity and slowly begin to catch on, Jesus tells them not to share the information with anyone (8:30; 9:9). Finally, when the title Messiah is applied to Jesus, he quickly changes the title to the "Son of Man" (8:29–31; 14:61–62). Mark clearly cannot reveal the identity of Jesus until all the evidence is in place. The key piece of evidence is the cross.

There are three titles that are central to Mark's understanding of Jesus' identity. First, there is the title Messiah/Christ. We have seen that Mark backs away from this designation until he is able to refashion its meaning in the light of the passion narrative. The notions of kingship and political deliverance that the tradition had tied so closely to this title cannot mean the same thing in the world of the kingdom of God. In Mark's mind, power is meant for service and for giving life to others. Any other use of power saps it of its vitality and distorts it.

Secondly, Mark believes Jesus is the apocalyptic Son of Man foretold in Daniel 7:13 and developed in certain parts of the non-canonical apocalyptic literature. The tradition held that the Son of Man would come at the end of time, judge the false worlds and empires that human beings have built for themselves, and establish the kingdom of God. While this title is close to the heart of the gospel, Mark must also rework it. He does so in the eighth section of the gospel in the passion predictions. There he reveals that the Son of Man must suffer, die, and rise again. The Son of Man brings the kingdom to God's people, but he does so by giving himself for others.

The key title for Mark, however, is Son of God. At first only supernatural beings know that Jesus is the Son of God. The demons know, but they are not allowed to reveal it (3:11–12; 5:7). The voice from heaven at the baptism and the transfiguration uses this title for Jesus. But at the baptism the voice speaks only to Jesus, and after the transfiguration Jesus warns the disciples not to disclose what they have heard. The only human voice in the narrative to call Jesus by this title is the centurion who witnessed his death. Only after Jesus has given his life for others can human beings begin to comprehend who Jesus truly is.

Mark lived long before the Council of Nicea. That council met in the year 325 and defined the dogma that Jesus is the Son of God and shares the same divine nature and being as God the Father. Nicea met two and one-half centuries after Mark wrote his gospel. It would be anachronistic to think that Mark had the dogmatic statement of Nicea in mind when he calls Jesus the Son of God. Mark does not think about Jesus in theoretical terms that contemplate what natures Jesus might possess. Mark thinks practically, not theoretically. He knows that divine power resides in Jesus and that the Spirit of God was upon him. Mark's teaching about Jesus is part of a tradition that will lead the disciples of Jesus to declare at Nicea in 325 that Jesus is God, the Son, who shares all that God the Father is. Mark's understanding that divine power worked through Jesus raised questions for later Christians about exactly who Jesus must be in order to wield such power. Although Mark wrote long before the Nicene bishops and theologians made clear the doctrine of the divinity of Jesus, Mark held the same faith in Jesus as the Nicene fathers. That faith would take time to develop in its understanding and expression, but Mark's gospel is an essential building block in that process of development.

As we stand in front of the text and reflect upon the picture of Jesus that Mark presents to us, we must rethink the idea of divinity. Our usual approach to defining God is philosophical. We take the attributes of the world and of our humanity that we think are most valuable and remove the limits from them and apply them to God analogically. Thus God is all-powerful, all-knowing, all-wise, all-loving. God is not bound by time and space and thus eternal and present everywhere. Christian doctrine, however, tells us that the greatest clue we have to the nature of God is not what creation and humanity tell us about our creator, but the very human story of Jesus. Divinity and humanity are joined in Jesus in such a way that his humanity reveals the hidden nature of God.

The cross remains the central clue to the identity of Jesus. It is the central revelation of God in human history. It tells us that the nature of God is to pour out life for the sake of the other. This giving of life to each other defines the relationship of the Father and the Son through all eternity. The Nicene Creed states that the Son is eternally begotten of the Father, that their eternal relationship consists of the Father's eternally and totally sharing his being and his life with the Son. That relationship of giving life makes them God. John in his First Epistle states that God is love (4:16). God is not one who loves or one who is loved. The very nature of God is life-giving love itself.

When people give of what they have (bread) or give of their very selves (their lives) for the sake of others, they realize the kingdom. To enter into the kingdom is to enter into the very life and dynamics of what the Father and the Son share in the divine nature. The early Greek Fathers of the Church insisted that we are saved by coming to participate in the divine nature and the divine life. Although Mark never says this, his work is part of the tradition that will lead Christians to this insight. The central mystery of the gospel is not only that the kingdom comes when we give of our lives for the sake of others, but that in doing so we come to share the eternal life of God.

Key Points for Preaching

We do not preach often on the passion narrative of Mark's gospel. We read it in the liturgy in its entirety only on Palm Sunday of Year B, and then only in conjunction with the reading of the story of Jesus' entry into Jerusalem, the blessing of palms, and the procession. Palm Sunday homilies tend to be short.

But hidden deep in all of our preaching lie certain assumptions about the nature of God, how God works in our lives, and how God has redeemed us through the death and resurrection of God's son. Mark's passion narrative asks us to think deeply about those assumptions. Mark assumes that we cannot begin to talk about Jesus as God's son until we have seen him give his life on the cross. Language about God that centers on such attributes as almighty and all-knowing comes up short before the mystery of God revealed in the cross. The God who empties himself and enters into our suffering and struggles takes center stage. The cross reveals the central attribute of God as one who gives his life to and for others. This view of God should mark not just our preaching on the story of the death of Jesus, but also the view of God that we take in all our preaching.

We also make deep assumptions about how the cross of Jesus saves us. Far too often we see redemption as a legal transaction in which penalties are paid so that forgiveness might be ours. Again Mark challenges us to think differently. He asks us to think how the giving of life for another can reflect divine power and be healing. He wants us to consider the basic dynamics of life: hoarded for the self, life withers away, but given for others it yields into an immense harvest. Mark has shown us this dynamic at work through the entire ministry of Jesus. In the passion narrative he gives it full expression. The cross is not a legal transaction; it is God breathing his life into the world once again.

Mark has given homilists a wonderful opportunity to invite people to think of God and God's saving work in a new way. More than that, Mark allows the homilist to invite the people of God to enter into the life of God in new and deeper ways. Christians enter the life of God through the cross. The entrance lies not in some divine courtroom where sin is judged and its proper punishment meted out. The entrance is in our homes where families give life to each other in the love that they share. It is in our places of work if we can but see our jobs as service to others. We enter through our friendships, through our willingness to share life's struggles and pain with each other, through the ministries we carry out for the sake of those in need. We enter God's life by entering more fully into human life.

CHAPTER TWELVE

TO BEGIN AGAIN

Mark 16:1–8

Let the river run,
Let all the dreamers
Wake the nations.
Come, the New Jerusalem.

Carly Simon, "Let the River Run"

The World of the Text

The best manuscripts of Mark's gospel have no appearances of the risen Lord. The women go to Jesus' tomb early on the first day of the week, bearing spices they have purchased to anoint the body. They find the tomb open and a man dressed in white sitting inside. He tells them Jesus is not there, that he has risen and will go ahead of them to Galilee. They are to announce this news to Peter and the disciples and tell them they will see the risen Lord in Galilee. The women flee in terror and amazement and say nothing to anyone. Fear has gripped them.

The gospel ends abruptly at this point. Later editors have added other endings, but these do not share Mark's vocabulary or style. They read like summaries of the stories of the risen Jesus told by the other gospel writers. Mark must have known these stories, for they circulated through the Christian communities of the first century. But he chose not to include them in his gospel.

This report of the resurrection of Jesus picks up on several important themes of the gospel. It brings to fulfillment the predictions of Jesus in the eighth section of the gospel in which he foretold not only his death but also his being raised. It strongly confirms the central mystery of the gospel, that a person finds life in abundance by giving life to others. But most importantly, it repeats the theme of the disciples' struggle to follow Jesus. Fear overwhelms the women, and they do not carry out the instructions given by the man dressed in white. The gospel ends on a question mark. It leaves the reader wondering how the gospel went any further when it seemed to be choked by the fears of those to whom it has been entrusted.

The gospel, however, has something of a circular structure. This last story points back to Galilee where the gospel began. The women are to tell Peter and the other disciples that Jesus will meet them there. There is a certain ambiguity in this instruction. The figure at the tomb could be pointing to the second coming of Jesus and the arrival of the fullness of the kingdom of God at the end of time. Mark expects this return of Jesus soon, within the lifetime of the generation for whom he writes his gospel. Perhaps he sees Galilee as the place where the kingdom will arrive in its fullness just as it began to unfold in the opening section of the gospel. Mark does not concentrate on resurrection appearances because the coming of the end of time remains crucial in his mind. The resurrection of the Lord is but a step on the way to the full realization of the promises of God.

On the other hand, Mark may be addressing the reader, who, having heard the gospel, now stands trembling like the women at the tomb. Will the reader have faith in the promises of the kingdom? Will the reader live as if the promises of God were possible and the world of the kingdom of God on the horizon? Will the reader be willing to give his or her life for the sake of others as the only way that the promises can be realized? If the reader casts about with uncertainty, Mark points them back to Galilee, back to where the gospel began, and invites them to move through the clues again so that they might break open the mystery of the kingdom of God.

Reflections in Front of the Text

Apostolicity is one of the four marks of the church, which we profess in the Nicene Creed to be one, holy, catholic, and apostolic. In its most basic sense, apostolicity means that our faith depends upon the testimony of the apostles and the tradition the Christian community has handed down from them through the centuries. The apostles serve as the witnesses of the ministry and teaching of Jesus. In part, we know Jesus because of them. Our encounters with the Lord depend to some degree on that first generation of witnesses. We have not encountered the risen Lord in the same way that they did when they saw him, talked with him, and shared meals with him.

Mark recognizes our dependence on the witness of the apostles and therefore does not tell stories of the appearances of the risen Jesus. The ending of his gospel reflects the experience of his first-century community and those of us who have read his gospel down through the centuries. We have heard the reports that the Lord is risen, but we must take it on faith. Mark closes his gospel by placing us, his readers, exactly back at the beginning of the gospel. We have heard the promises, but what will we do with them? Like the women at the tomb on Easter Sunday, we too have fears that might cause us to say nothing to anyone about the gospel that Mark has proclaimed. We may fear letting go of our possessions, our energy and time, our life for the sake of others, for we may be left with empty hands. We may fear relinquishing an old, familiar world in which we know how business, government, friendship and family work. The new world of the kingdom may seem like unexplored territory. But the angel at the tomb has assured us that Jesus has gone before us into Galilee, that Jesus has shown us the way to the kingdom and invited us to follow him.

Points for Preaching

Hope places us between two worlds. The world of the status quo we know quite well, the world where disease and injustice overwhelm people. In this world death often appears to have the last word. In this world many people are possessed by the things they think will make them happy. The other world inaugurates the kingdom of God with its promises of healing, justice, and the conquest of evil. But we only have small seeds, small foretastes of the fullness of that kingdom. At the end of the gospel Mark leaves us between these two worlds with the clues we need to understand the kingdom and how God realizes it in our lives and society. But he also knows that the truth of the kingdom can only be known by taking the risk of dying to self and finding life in giving it to others. Only by taking such a risk can we know that the promises of the kingdom are true. The kingdom sits on the horizon. As Carly Simon's lyrics proclaim: "Let all the dreamers wake the nations. Come, the new Jerusalem."

WORKS CITED

Berger, Peter L. and Thomas Luckman. *The Social Construction of Reality: A Treatise in the Sociology of Knowledge*. New York: Doubleday and Company, 1966.

Eliade, Mircea. *Myth and Reality*. New York: Harper Torchbooks, 1963.

———. *The Myth of the Eternal Return, or Cosmos and History*. Princeton, N.J.: Princeton University Press, 1954.

Küng, Hans. *On Being a Christian*. New York: Doubleday and Company, Inc., 1976.

Moltmann, Jürgen. *The Crucified God*. New York: Harper and Row Publishers, 1974.

National Conference of Catholic Bishops. *Economic Justice for All*. Washington, D.C.: National Conference of Catholic Bishops, 1986.

Pope Paul VI. *Populorum Progressio* (March 26, 1967); *Octogesima Adveniens* (May 14, 1971).

Rahner, Karl. *Foundations of Christian Faith: An Introduction to the Idea of Christianity*. New York: The Seabury Press, 1978.

———. "The Life of the Dead," *Theological Investigations, Volume IV: More Recent Writings*. Baltimore: Helicon Press, 1966.

Saint Augustine. *The Confessions*; translated Maria Boulding, O.S.B. Hyde Park: New City Press, 1997.

Tillich, Paul. *Systematic Theology, Volume One* and *Systematic Theology, Volume Two*. New York: University of Chicago Press, 1957.